THE BOOK
OF THE
EARTHWORM

Sally Coulthard is a bestselling author whose
titles include *The Little Book of Building
Fires*, *The Little Book of Snow*, *The Hedgehog
Handbook*, *The Bee Bible* and *A Short History
of the World According to Sheep*. She also
writes about rural life, craft and design.
She lives in North Yorkshire.

An Apollo book

First published in the UK in 2021 by Head of Zeus Ltd

9 7 5 3 1 2 4 6 8

A catalogue record for this book is available from
the British Library.

ISBN (HB): 9781789544756
ISBN (E): 9781789544749

Typeset by Kelly-Anne Levey
Linocuts © Sarah Price

Printed and bound in Germany
by CPI Books GmbH, Leck

Head of Zeus Ltd
First Floor East
5–8 Hardwick Street
London EC1R 4RG
www.headofzeus .com

THE BOOK
OF THE
EARTHWORM

SALLY
COULTHARD

An Apollo Book

CONTENTS

Earthworm behaviour 83

...love for all living creatures, the most noble attribute of man.

Charles Darwin, *The Descent of Man* (1871)

Introduction

When Charles Darwin had to pick what he thought was the most important animal in the world, he didn't choose the ape for its intelligence, or the sheep for its usefulness, or the duck-billed platypus for its sheer oddness. He chose the earthworm.

Calling it 'nature's plough', Darwin crowned the humble earthworm the most significant creature on the planet, stating: 'It may be doubted whether there are many other animals which have played so important a part in the history of the world, as have these lowly organised creatures.' Two thousand years earlier, Greek philosopher Aristotle had hailed worms as the 'entrails of earth'.[*]

And yet, most of us know almost nothing about these marvellous engineers of the soil. We take them for granted, but without earthworms, life would stop. The world's soil would

---

[*] Aristotle never actually calls earthworms the 'intestines of the soil', as is often misquoted. *In De Generatione Animalium* (On the Generation of Animals), Book III, translated by Arthur Platt (1910), he writes: 'For all of these [animals], though they have but little blood by nature, are nevertheless sanguine, and have a heart with blood in it as the origin of the parts; and the so-called "entrails of earth".'

be barren – our gardens, fields and farms wouldn't be able to grow the food and support the crops and animals we need to survive. Earthworms not only recycle decaying plants, putting nutrients back into the soil, but also, with their endless wiggling and burrowing, they help rain soak away and provide food for wildlife as diverse as foxes and frogs. Recent research even suggests earthworms can help clean up polluted land, turning it back into rich, fertile ground.

Earthworms are heroes in miniature. Many of our current environmental issues can seem overwhelming and yet, ironically, some of the solutions may lie in one of nature's smallest, most overlooked creatures. For too long we have taken the endless toil of earthworms for granted, without really knowing who's doing all the work, or why.

Leonardo da Vinci famously declared: 'We know more about the movement of celestial bodies than about the soil underfoot.' Everyone should know what's going on under their back gardens. It's miraculous.

Earthworms and us

The tulip and the butterfly

Appear in gayer coats than I

Let me be dressed as fine as I will,

Flies, worms, and flowers, exceed me still.

Isaac Watts, *Divine Songs* (1715)

One of the most remarkable things about the earthworm is just how little we *really* know about this extraordinary creature. For one of the most important animals on the planet, it has been merrily ignored for much of its existence.

Until about thirty years ago, only a few dedicated scientists had ever studied this amazing organism, but in recent years an increasing number of people are waking up to just how critical earthworms are to our entire ecological system. In particular, people have been looking at the potential of earthworms in sustainable farming practices – such as vermiculture (getting worms to make fertiliser) and organic waste recycling – and, perhaps more surprisingly, as a source of high-protein food (see *Can you eat earthworms?* page 44).

Other research projects have investigated the role of earthworms in restoring polluting or degraded farmland and environmental monitoring. The earthworm, whether it likes it or not, has been dragged centre stage. Only now are we starting to learn just what a valuable creature the earthworm really is.

Perhaps the first thing to say is that there isn't just *one* type of earthworm. In fact, there are thousands. Across the world, there are thought to be at least 3,000 different species of earthworm, but because they've been so little studied, there are probably thousands more than that, tucked away and yet to be discovered.

Earthworms also come in a wide variety of sizes. Different species can range in length from a centimetre to a gigantic 3 metres. Their colours vary enormously, too – alongside the muted browns and pinks we are familiar with in our own back gardens, some earthworms are green, stripy red and even a gorgeous purply blue.

Did you know ?

The collective noun for earthworms is a 'clew'; clew is an ancient relic of the Old English *cliwen* and means 'ball of yarn or thread'. Other names for a group of worms include a mouthful, bed, clat, bunch and squirm.

THE THREE TYPES OF EARTHWORM

Who really respects the earthworm,
the farmworker far under the grass in the soil.
He keeps the earth always changing.
He works entirely full of soil,
speechless with soil, and blind.

Harry Edmund Martinson, *The Earthworm* (trans. Robert Bly)

For all their glorious variety, it's helpful to divide earthworms into three groups. These categories are roughly based on whereabouts in the soil the earthworm lives, and how it feeds and burrows. Starting from the surface, moving down into the soil, you'll discover:

SURFACE DWELLERS (Epigeic) – this group of earthworms doesn't actually live *in* the soil. Instead, it rummages around on the surface among moist, warm, decomposing leaves and organic matter. These earthworms feed on this decaying material and on the fungi and bacteria that help break it down. They tend to be small (around 3–4 centimetres long), don't burrow into the ground, and are often red or reddish brown in colour.

Earthworms in this category include the wonderfully stripy Tiger worms (*Eisenia fetida*), which often live in compost heaps and are also known as Redworms or Red Wrigglers. You don't find many of these worms on agricultural land because of the lack of any permanent leaf litter; they tend, instead, to prefer grasslands and forests.

SHALLOW BURROWERS (Endogeic) – this second group of earthworms lives in the soil but usually stays in the upper layers (to a depth of around 30 centimetres). They feed on the dead leaves, fungi and tiny creatures that are already mixed into that shallow layer of earth. Endogeic worms also burrow horizontally in the soil, creating a branch-like network of tunnels, and tend to be medium-sized (around 8–14 centimetres long) and very pale in colour (such as pinks, greens and blue-greys).

DEEP BURROWERS (Anecic) – this third group of earthworms is the largest in length and can dig as far as 3 metres down into the soil. They burrow in straight vertical lines – rather like an elevator shaft – coming up to the surface at night-time to grab plant material for food, which they pull down into their burrows. They are also red or brown in colour but usually have a darker head and lighter-coloured tail. These are also the earthworms that leave little heaps of soily poo on the surface of your lawn – these piles are called 'worm casts'.

Of all the deep burrowers, the best known is the Common earthworm (*Lumbricus terrestris*). This is the gardener's friend – also known as the lob worm, the night crawler, the granddaddy worm and the dew worm – and is the largest naturally occurring earthworm across most of Europe (around 9–30 centimetres). The body of the Common earthworm can be as thick as a pencil and its tail can be flattened into a paddle shape, to help the earthworm grip the sides of its burrow.

THE EARTHWORM COMMUNITY

In reality, nature is never tidy. The three categories of earthworm are useful but, out in the field, the boundaries between different species of earthworms can get a bit blurred. For example, compost worms – such as the stripy Tiger worms (*Eisenia fetida*) – are sometimes put into their own separate category, distinct from other surface-dwelling epigeic worms. Other worm experts like to separate shallow-burrowing earthworms into three distinct groups of their own, depending on how deep they live in the soil and what they eat.

Neat categories suit scientists in labs, but earthworm behaviour isn't entirely fixed; populations can, to a certain extent, adapt their behaviour according to their environment. This ecological plasticity means that the same species of earthworm can display different behaviours or morphological characteristics in different local environments. In the northern hemisphere, for example, the widely abundant Grey worm (*Aporrectodea caliginosa*) is a shallow burrower, making short, horizontal burrows. The same worm in the southern hemisphere makes long, vertical burrows, just like a Common earthworm (*Lumbricus terrestris*), and behaves more like a deep-burrowing species.

Few studies have managed to establish the ratio of earthworms we have in the soil – i.e., do we have more surface dwellers than deep burrowers? A Natural England survey,[1] however, attempted to find out what kinds of earthworms lived where.

By far the biggest group of earthworms was the shallow burrowers, making up around three-quarters of all the worms they found. Surface dwellers made up the next largest group – around a fifth of all the earthworms – and the deep burrowers just one in twenty. The different species of earthworms don't seem to bother each other – depending on the habitat, communities of up to fifteen different species of earthworm rub along nicely together, happily coexisting within the same ecological niche.[2]

The so-called Common earthworm, it turns out, isn't *that* common. For such a well-known earthworm, it would seem that it only accounts for about one in every eighty of the earthworms under our feet. The small, shallow-burrowing Grey worm, by contrast, made up over a third of the species found in the Natural England survey. You'll recognise a Grey worm if you see one – it's beautifully shaded, like a decorator's colour card, graduating from a red head through to a pale pink middle and a purply-grey tail.

RECORD-BREAKING EARTHWORMS

These worms seem to abound more in ground which is lightly tilled, than in such as has been well worked; but in lay ground they seem to be more numerous than any where else...

The Commercial Agricultural and Manufacturer's Magazine, Volume 6 (1802)

The largest Common earthworm (*Lumbricus terrestris*) ever recorded in the UK wriggled its way into the record books measuring 40 centimetres in length and weighed a meaty five times more than the average earthworm. 'Dave the Earthworm' was discovered in an English vegetable patch and is now permanently preserved for posterity in London's Natural History Museum's collection.

Dave, however, was a tiddler compared to the world's largest species. One of these is Australia's Giant Gippsland earthworm (*Megascolides australis*). Found only in the Bass River Valley in the south-eastern state of Victoria, this gentle giant measures, on average, a metre long and a chunky 2 centimetres in diameter. Giant Gippsland earthworms can live for five years or more, slowly pushing their way through the wet clay subsoils of riverbanks. The longer they live, the bigger they get; older specimens have been known to mature to drainpipe proportions of 3 metres.

The record for the longest earthworm ever found belongs to a species called the African Giant earthworm (*Microchaetus rappi*). In 1967, a huge specimen was found on a road between Alice and King William's Town, in South Africa. The average length of the *Micro-chaetus rappi* is usually around 1.8 metres, but this particular earthworm measured 6.7 metres long and 2 centimetres wide – the same length as the average height of a giraffe.

Earthworms seem to thrive and grow to larger sizes in undisturbed ground. A recent study found a large concentration of whoppers on the

Scottish Isle of Rum.[3] A team of scientists discovered that the tiny island, which is also a nature reserve, had one particular location where Common earthworms had an average weight of around 12 grams, which is *three times* heavier than Common earthworms in other parts of the UK. The protected habitat of the island, which has plentiful organic matter, also lacks many of the mammals that usually devour earthworms, such as badgers, moles or hedgehogs. The area where the earthworms were found also happened to have an unusually high number of blood-sucking parasitic ticks, which discouraged people from ever attempting to settle and farm the land. Left alone, unchallenged by human activity or predation, the Rum earthworms could grow older, and subsequently larger, than in any other part of the country.

Did you know

The World Record for 'Most Worms Charmed' at the World Worm Charming Championships was 567 in half an hour and achieved, rather brilliantly, by a ten-year-old girl called Sophie Smith.

WHEN DID EARTHWORMS EVOLVE?

When dinosaurs were crashing around on the surface of the Earth, the lowly earthworm was already wriggling around underneath their feet. Recent analysis has discovered that the common ancestor to all earthworms lived at least 209 million years ago.

At this time, the world didn't have seven separate continents, but rather one massive supercontinent called Pangaea. When this vast, consolidated land mass began to split apart – about 180 million years ago – earthworms were carried off to the furthest reaches of the planet and evolved into the thousands of different species we see today. Antarctica is the only continent that doesn't currently have a species of earthworm, although earthworms probably did once live there until the continent's drift southwards made the land too cold for them to survive.

Continental Europe has about two hundred different species. Britain by itself doesn't have a vast number of native earthworms – twenty-six species at the last count. It's thought that during the last Ice Age, the existing earthworms in Britain were killed off. When the glaciers finally retreated, earthworms from the warmer parts of Europe began to move northwards, eventually reaching Britain by crossing the land bridge that then connected the east coast to the European mainland. So, all Britain's earthworms are, in fact, European.

WOULD HUMANS SURVIVE IF WORMS WENT EXTINCT?

The nation that destroys its soils destroys itself.

Franklin D. Roosevelt, Letter to all State Governors
on a Uniform Soil Conservation Law (1937)

Earthworms, rather like bees, are one of the groups of animals known as 'keystone species'. They have such a profound effect on our ecology that, without them, humans would struggle to survive.

Modern agriculture relies on healthy, productive soil. From growing cereals, fruit and vegetables to industrial crops such as biofuels, fibre for clothing and animal feeds – good soil supports it all. Even some of the things we might not first think of – from paper to pharmaceuticals – started

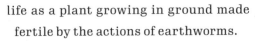

life as a plant growing in ground made fertile by the actions of earthworms.

Without earthworms, the soil would die. They play a crucial role in breaking down organic matter (such as dead leaves and flowers) and putting that goodness back into the soil. Thanks to their constant eating and pooing, earthworms release the nutrients in organic matter by breaking it down into tiny pieces, making it available for use by living plants, fungi and bacteria. An estimated 3.5×10^{10} (35 billion) tonnes of terrestrial leaf litter are turned over worldwide each year in soils.[4]

As they wriggle and squirm underground, earthworms also aerate the soil, leaving it light and fluffy. Their constant burrowing creates air pockets, through which water can drain. Without this sponge-like texture, soil soon becomes compacted and prone to flooding. This never-ending churning and ploughing also helps bring nutrients that are deep in the soil back up to the surface, where plants can easily access them. Scientific experiments have shown, for example, that earthworms increase plant growth by, on average, 20 per cent[5] in comparison to plants growing in soils with no earthworms.

In fact, earthworms do such an incredible job at improving the soil in our gardens that they actually *help* plants resist attack from other pests. Studies have shown that earthworms boost the nutritional value plants get from the soil, enabling them to better defend themselves against the insects and herbivores who eat them. Plants that are constantly damaged by insects or herbivores try to protect themselves by changing the chemical composition of their leaves. When the nutrition of the plant is improved by earthworm activity, the plant can produce more of these defensive compounds. In one experiment, for example, where invasive Spanish slugs (*Arion vulgaris*) were introduced to micro-ecosystems to monitor how much damage they would do, the sites where earthworms were present reduced the number of leaves damaged by 60 per cent.[6]

EARTHWORMS
AND SEEDS

Earthworms also have an interesting role to play in seed germination. Soil is full of seeds; when plants drop their seeds, not all of them will germinate straight away. Depending on where they land, seeds will either grow, rot or go into dormancy, waiting for the right conditions to thrive. The seeds in this last category inevitably get covered over and worked into the soil, where they can persist for years. It's a clever strategy and means that plants can survive, in the form of an underground 'seed bank', even if conditions above ground won't support them.

Studies have shown that some species of earthworms eat seeds as they chomp through the soil and leaf litter. By ingesting seeds, and then depositing them on the soil surface in their casts, earthworms are one of the main ways seeds get a chance to come back to the soil surface and grow. Scientists have also shown that seeds that have passed through the guts of an earthworm have a better chance of germinating than seeds that haven't – the chemical composition of worm casts seems to give seeds a better chance of germinating.[7] A reverse effect is also beneficial – by burying seeds through their day-to-day activity, earthworms may be key to the formation of large seed banks in many different ecosystems.

ARE EARTHWORMS IN TROUBLE?

To forget how to dig the earth and tend the soil
is to forget ourselves.

Gandhi

Some earthworms are having a rough time. Unlike nature's more dazzling, attention-grabbing species, the earthworm and its story have gone largely unnoticed. Some of the more exotic species – such as Australia's Giant Gippsland earthworm (*Megascolides australis*) – are endangered, thanks in most part to habitat loss. And the picture isn't too rosy elsewhere.

Studies have shown that, overall, numbers of earthworms are declining in certain areas, especially those regions that are intensively farmed. No one quite knows what's happening, but researchers suspect that excessive tillage (the mechanised digging and turning of soil), certain types of crops, microplastics in the soil and the overuse of pesticides could play a huge role in the decrease.

In a recent scientific study of English agricultural land, for example, nearly half of the land surveyed was seriously deficient in earthworms. Roughly 1,300 hectares of farmed land was studied in total. Over 40 per cent of fields had 'poor earthworm biodiversity' – meaning very few or no surface-dwelling and deep-burrowing worms were found. And while most fields had healthy numbers of shallow-burrowing earthworms, a fifth of all fields had no surface-dwelling worms and about one in six fields had no deep burrowers at all.

The farmers involved in the study, who did most of the surveying, were so alarmed by the results that over half of them pledged to change their soil management practices as a result.[8] Similar findings have been recorded across Europe – in Slovakia, for example, one study found the density of earthworms was nearly twice as high in the soil under permanent grassland compared to agricultural land.[9]

But the situation is not all bad. Habitats such as pasture and gardens seem to be supporting high numbers of earthworms. A citizen science count by Earthworm Watch, for example, recently found densities of 200 earthworms per metre which, if extrapolated out to the average UK home, could mean we each have over 32,000 earthworms in the everyday back garden.

HOW DOES A DECLINE IN EARTHWORMS AFFECT US?

While it's brilliant that suburban gardens and grass-land are havens for earthworms, the situation for farmland is a serious one. Fewer earthworms means lower soil fertility, which in turn equals lower crop yields – a real problem in terms of food security for the world's growing population.

Poor soil fertility also produces less nutritious plants – a 2004 study published in *Scientific American* compared nutrients in crops and vegetables grown in the 1950s with those grown at the turn of the millennium and revealed significant drops in levels of protein, calcium, phosphorus, iron, vitamin B2 and vitamin C.[10]

A decline in the number of earthworms also affects the wildlife that relies on them for food; the song thrush population, for example, has plummeted in recent years, a crash thought to be due, at least in part, to an absence of earthworms to feed their young in springtime. Fewer worms means that baby chicks either starve in the nest or fail to thrive after they leave. Without earthworms, other wildlife such as hedgehogs, foxes, robins, shrews, moles, wood mice and badgers also struggle to find enough food. Earthworms, for instance, make up about 60 per cent of a badger's diet, while the American robin can catch 4 metres' worth in a single day.

A recent study also found that long-term pesticide use seems to be having a direct effect on earthworms. A Danish/French research collaboration discovered that agricultural pesticides, used on crops, are stunting the growth of earthworms and causing a drop in their ability to reproduce. The scientists involved in the study found that, although earthworms can tolerate a certain level of pesticides and fungicides in the soil and have developed strategies to detoxify themselves, this behaviour comes at a cost. It takes a huge amount of energy for the earthworm's system to be constantly ridding itself of toxic chemicals – the result is that earthworms in heavily sprayed areas suffer from stunted growth and are less successful at breeding.[11]

Fewer earthworms also means that soil can get very compacted. If agricultural land can't absorb rainwater, the run-off ends up in local watercourses. This flow is often contaminated with pesticides, nitrates and other chemicals, which, if it trickles into streams and rivers, causes a great deal of harm to aquatic wildlife. For soil to absorb water effectively, earthworm burrows need to connect to one another like a huge network of drains – research has shown that tillage can significantly damage these water conduits, stopping them from working. Other agricultural activities, such as the overuse of pesticides, have also been shown to affect how quickly soil can absorb water, because of increased earthworm mortality.

It might not seem much of a problem if earthworm burrows are damaged and don't drain as effectively, but flooding can cause untold misery to communities and the people whose homes, public spaces and services are ruined when rainwater has nowhere to go. Soil that is full of earthworm tunnels is less likely to flash flood; when you consider that more people are killed in the US by flooding each year than by tornadoes, hurricanes or lightning,[12] the ecological significance of the lowly earthworm is thrown into stark relief.

Alongside intensive agriculture, there's a rather more exotic threat to earthworms. Certain species of flatworms – particularly New Zealand's *Arthurdendyus tri-angulatus* – pose a serious threat to European populations of native earthworms. These tiny ribbon-like creatures originally landed on European shores by accident, hidden in the soil of gardeners' pot plants. Slim and very stretchy, this particular flatworm seems to love eating earthworms, which it devours by first wrapping itself around the worm and then liquidising it by secreting digestive enzymes. Researchers have found that one flatworm can wolf its way through fourteen earthworms a week and, even after it has decimated an earthworm population in a particular place, can survive for up to a year waiting for the earthworm numbers to improve, so it can once again resume its assault.

A recent study also found a new and unexpected challenge to earthworm health – microplastics in the soil.[13] These are pieces of plastic less than 5 millimetres in size; they are absolutely everywhere, widely distributed in our seas and in our soils. They come from two sources – one is 'primary microplastics', such as microfibres, microbeads and pellets that enter the environment as tiny fragments. The other source is larger pieces of plastic – such as plastic bottles, carrier bags and packaging – that, over time, degrade and break down into minuscule pieces. No one had studied the effect of these microplastics on earthworms until this research

FEED THE WORMS

• The more organic matter you can add to your soil, the more earthworms you'll have. Under natural, 'wild' conditions, the condition of the soil tends to stay fairly even – the year-round cycle of growth and decay ensures that enough organic matter is reincorporated into the soil, along with animal droppings and decomposing creatures.

• In gardens and other growing spaces such as allotments, we tend to take more goodness out of the soil than we put in. We tidy up fallen leaves, pull out dead plants and clear away the natural debris left behind at the end of the season – all the things that would ordinarily contribute to the richness of the soil.

• There are a number of ways to add organic matter to soil – home-made compost (see *How to help earthworms #3* page 52), shop-bought compost, municipal compost (from council-run recycling centres), mushroom compost from commercial growers, spent hops from breweries, well-rotted manure, spent coffee grounds, leaf mould and composted bark.

• Apply organic material in spring, before the growing season starts – gardening bodies usually recommend applying organic matter at least 5 centimetres deep but even just a generous sprinkling will help improve the nutrition in the soil for earthworms. Keep adding extra compost every year.

project looked into the problem. Surface-dwelling earthworms (*Eisenia fetida*) were exposed to soil that contained minute amounts of fluorescent polystyrene microplastics over a two-week period. Even at very low concentrations, the results showed that the earthworms suffered both cell and DNA damage from exposure to microplastics.

WHAT'S WORM-FRIENDLY FARMING?

Who are the farmer's servants? …
Geology and Chemistry, the quarry of the air,
the water of the brook, the lightning of the cloud,
the castings of the worm, the plough of the frost.

Ralph Waldo Emerson, from '*Farming*' in *Society and Solitude* (1870)

The same principles for keeping garden earthworms happy apply to farmed land; they need plenty of decaying plant matter to feed on and minimum disturbance.

If a farming system constantly removes all crop residues before they are recycled back into the soil, earthworms will struggle to find anything to eat. If we can find a way to increase the amount of organic material that gets left on agricultural land, either through crop stubble, using green manures such as clover or vetch that act as a mulch, crop rotations that add organic matter to the soil, or even switching some arable land to permanent pasture, all these measures would increase the amount of plant material available to earthworms.

Digging and turning soil, especially on a large mechanical scale, also creates a number of problems for earthworms – it destroys their burrows, displaces their cocoons, and often brings them to the surface, where they either die from UV exposure or desiccation, or get gobbled up. The constant turning of soil also tends to dry it out – a disaster for creatures that need moist soil. Practices such as no-till agriculture, leaving behind crop residues, planting cover crops and using no-drill equipment are all being tested as ways to improve soil health and bring back earthworm numbers.

It's unfair to blame farmers. We all have a role to play. Downward pressure on prices, encouraged by consumers wanting cheaper food, has forced farmers to increase their output while reducing inputs. This approach is exacerbated by issues such as short-term tenancies, which don't allow farmers to think long-term about their land, and the demand for energy crops such as maize, which can exacerbate soil degradation. There's also been little in terms of education, government incentives or national policy to help farmers to get the right advice and access to new methods and equipment.

DO EARTHWORMS AFFECT CLIMATE CHANGE?

The health of soil, plant, animal and man is one and indivisible.

Sir Albert Howard (1873-1947)

In recent years it was thought that earthworms might be actually *contributing* to greenhouse gas emissions. As earthworms go about their business, turning over soil, scientists wondered whether they were releasing carbon dioxide that was trapped in the soil into the atmosphere.

Soil acts as a huge storage system for carbon, which is pulled out of the air by plants and transported by their roots into the soil. When soil is dug up, turned over and tilled, it speeds up the release of carbon back into the atmosphere. It was thought that, because earthworms churn up soil, they might also be speeding up this carbon-release process.

However, new studies have shown that earthworms actually *help* stabilise carbon into a form that is more likely to stay in the soil. As soil passes through an earthworm's digestive system, the soil carbon is converted into a form that is more resistant to decay. Once it has come out of the other end of the worm, the soil also has a crumblier structure, which not only helps to hold on to the carbon, but also makes more plants grow, which in turn pull more carbon from the atmosphere.

Other research has shown that deep-burrowing earthworms actually change the distribution of carbon in the soil, dragging it further down underground. When soil carbon is near the surface, it's very vulnerable to being released when the soil is tilled. Deep-burrowing earthworms move the carbon from the surface soil and take it to the deep subsoil, where it is much less likely to be disturbed.

EARTHWORMS AND
SPACE TRAVEL

While we've yet to find life on other planets, that doesn't mean earthworms won't play their part in space exploration. One of the most interesting recent experiments involving earthworms involved trying to see if they could survive in soil similar to that found on Mars. If humans want to live on the 'Red Planet', working out how to grow crops on Mars will be one of our biggest challenges. Scientists believe the only way to do this will be to modify the planet's soil, which is sterile and full of toxic compounds.

One fascinating piece of research not only managed to keep earthworms alive in the simulated Mars soil, but the worms actually started to reproduce and produce new baby worms. The key to any self-sustaining agricultural system in outer space would have to revolve around the recycling of nutrients – from plant and human waste – back into the soil. Earthworms, NASA believes, will be critical to this process. The next stage in the study is going to investigate what kinds of bacteria and fungi will be able to cope in Mars' soil and, crucially, how crops will be pollinated. The bumble bee is next on the research list.

Space travel also uncovered another scientific puzzle back down on Earth. First described by scientists in the 1940s but well known by locals, the wetlands around the Orinoco river in South America are studded with strange mounds of earth. Known as 'surales' by the native population, no one could explain how this vast mosaic of regularly spaced, bizarrely uniform mounds came into being – they cover 29,000 square miles and can reach up to 2 metres high and 5 metres wide. Only from space could the true extent of the surales be seen and yet no one, until recently, could explain their presence. Giant earthworms turn out to be the culprits, creating huge piles of worm casts as they dig through the waterlogged soil.

WHY ARE WORMS
CALLED 'WORMS'?

Then the worm woke; cause of strife was renewed:
for then he moved over the stones, hard-hearted
beheld his foe's footprints...

Beowulf (trans. T. Donaldson)

'Worm' is an ancient word but throughout time its meaning has shifted. In Anglo-Saxon, or Old English, worm or 'wyrm' was a general word for any creature that crawled, wriggled or slithered its way around. Such a broad category meant that frogs, snails, snakes, scorpions, earthworms and many other unrelated animals came into the same category. What unified them all, however, was their unpopularity. 'Wyrms' were creatures viewed as noxious, repulsive and dangerous – 'vermin' comes from the same root and we still use it to describe troublesome pests.

'Wyrm' also extended to include mythical animals – creatures sent to torment the soul, demons that lived in the underworld and terrifying serpents. The word was even used to describe dragons and dragon-like creatures, legendary animals in European folklore who terrorised villagers and devoured livestock. Even Shakespeare uses its archaic meaning in *Antony and Cleopatra*, when the eponymous queen refers to the poisonous asp as 'the pretty worm of Nilus that kills and pains not'.

Did you know ?

The Latin name for the Common earthworm – *Lumbricus terrestris* – has an even stranger beginning. The origin of 'lumbricus' as a word used to describe an earthworm is unclear – one possibility is that it is connected to the Latin *umbilicus*, meaning 'navel' (hence 'umbilical cord') and an ancient belief that earthworms and intestinal worms were one and the same species.

WHY WAS DARWIN FASCINATED WITH EARTHWORMS?

In the last years of his life, Charles Darwin decided he wanted to write a book about earthworms. While most of his scientific colleagues thought Darwin's new topic a little unglamorous for one of the world's most eminent biologists, Darwin had long been fascinated by this 'unsung creature which, in its untold millions, transformed the land'.

It was a daring choice of subject in many ways, not least because, during the eighteenth and nineteenth centuries, earthworms were considered to be a nuisance, a troublesome garden pest that needed to be purged from the soil. François Rozier's *Complete Course of Agriculture*, written in the second half of the eighteenth century, made it abundantly clear that earthworms were noxious creatures that needed eliminating by any means possible: 'Every cultivator... knows the damage that worms do to seeds... it is thus advantageous to know the means to destroy them.' He goes on to present a comprehensive list of ways to remove and kill earthworms, including going out in the dead of night with a lantern to collect them in silence, whacking the ground with a mallet until they surface, hammering a stake into the ground and shaking it till the worms appear, and pouring various toxic infusions on to the soil.[†] Farmers were also vehemently anti-earthworm, blaming them for damage to crops. Turnip farmer Henry Vagg, for example, wrote to the *Hampshire Chronicle* in 1788, furious about the wrigglers destroying his valuable turnip plugs: 'The common earthworm by its

---

[†] Rozier met his own, rather sticky end, when he was blown up by a bomb during the Siege of Lyons during the French Revolution.

working, makes ground light and hollow about the plants, in consequence of which they are liable to be injured.' Henry went on to boast that his solution was to repeatedly roll and squash the soil down, a technique at odds with everything we now know about the harmful effects of soil compaction.

Darwin was unperturbed, however, by growers' disdain for the earthworm. His book, which was published in 1881, was the result of forty years' worth of observations of the Common earthworm (*Lumbricus terrestris*). He called it *The*  *Formation of Vegetable Mould through the Action of Worms, with Observations on their Habits*, although this was often shortened to just *Worms*. For such a lowly subject, the book was a hit. Even though Darwin himself described it as a 'small book of little moment', in its first month alone it sold 3,500 copies. Three years later nearly 9,000 copies of the book had been snapped up, more than equalling his other literary successes, including *On the Origin of Species*. Even Darwin was stunned by the interest in his book; in a letter to the geologist Mellard Reade, dated 8 November 1881, he enthused: 'It has been a complete surprise to me how many persons have cared for the subject.' In the same month, he wrote again, this time to another friend, the botanist

William Thiselton-Dyer: 'My book has been received with almost laughable enthusiasm, and 3,500 copies have been sold!!'

One of the reasons Darwin gave for wanting to study earthworms is perhaps surprising. For a scientist, he was also deeply philosophical – in his view, it was the smallest creatures, the seemingly insignificant, that held the key to nature's most spectacular processes. The original idea for the project, however, came from his uncle Josiah Wedgwood II (son of the English potter), who wanted Darwin to explain why the organic material he put down on his garden soil slowly disappeared over time.

Wedgwood had a hunch it might be earthworms, but it was Darwin, and his experiments, that finally solved the mystery. He placed his now famous 'worm stone' on the ground – just a round wheel of stone with a central peg for measuring – and charted its slow submersion into the ground over years. Darwin realised that as earthworms moved through the soil, they deposited new soil on the surface, causing whatever is sitting on the surface – whether it's small pebbles or vast megaliths – to slowly sink.

Darwin was also inherently fascinated and

thrilled by earthworms' behaviour. He was one of the first scientists to suggest they might have social relationships (see *Do Worms Make Friends?* page 125), food preferences, aversion to bright light and sensitivity to vibrations; and he even suspected that the earthworm had some kind of basic intelligence. He watched with delight as the earthworms in his experiments selected and pulled leaves into their burrows, based on shape. More often than not, the earthworms would pull the leaf from its more pointed end, allowing it to fit more easily into the burrow. Investigating further, Darwin cut up pieces of paper into narrow isosceles triangles to see if the earthworms would grab those by their 'sharpest' end; again the earthworms would, in the majority of cases, tug the tiny triangles from their apex, the end most likely to fit into their burrow. Amazed, Darwin noted that: 'If worms have a notion, however rude, of the shape of an object and of their burrows, as seems to be the case, they deserve to be called intelligent; for they then act in nearly the same manner as would a man under similar circumstances' (see also *Can You Train a Worm?* page 118).

NO DIG

• Earthworms hate being disturbed. The endless digging and tilling of soil not only disrupts their natural behaviour (and risks chopping worms in two) but also destroys their burrows. The constant cultivation and turning over of soil also crashes through the delicate soil ecosystem – in just one handful of soil there are more living organisms than all the humans on the planet. Billions of micro-organisms such as bacteria, algae, fungi and nematodes work furiously away in a living, breathing underground community that's home to a quarter of all life on Earth. Churning up soil is like taking a bulldozer to a rainforest, and exposes these micro-organisms to the damaging effects of UV light and dry air, destroying the balance and, in the end, making soil less fertile or productive.

- In general, you shouldn't need to aerate soil – earthworms will do that for you. They'll also drag organic matter on the soil surface down on your behalf. If you must dig, use a fork if possible. It's also important not to compact the soil by walking over it – practical solutions such as making stepping stones, wooden  walkways, raised beds, garden paths and not making overly wide beds all avoid the problem.

CAN YOU EAT EARTHWORMS?

Nobody loves me. I'm going into the garden
to eat worms.

Anon, early 20th century

For the Makiritare people of Venezuela, earthworms are a lifeline. They eat two different species, *Andiorrhinus kuru* and *Andiorrhinus motto*, both of which contain large amounts of high-quality protein comparable with levels in cows' milk and eggs. The earthworms are also packed with amino acids, fatty acids, minerals and trace elements, including generous amounts of calcium and iron (ten times more iron than soya beans).[14]

To make the earthworms palatable, the Makiritare either cook them in hot, but not boiling water (60–80°C) or, for a real treat, smoke them over a wood fire. In fact, the smoked earthworms are considered such a delicacy that they command three times the price of smoked fish or meats. The Maori of New Zealand, Australian Aborigines and nomadic Papua New Guineans also traditionally incorporated earthworms into their diet.

Looking towards the future, there is real appetite for new sources of sustainable protein. Scientists have been looking into the use of earthworms as human food and as an animal feed – farming invertebrates may be one way to assure food security over the next century and counteract the worst environmental excesses of the global livestock industry. It's currently possible to buy products such as dried earthworm or earthworm jerky as ready-to-eat snacks, or earthworm flour, which can be used as a protein-boosting ingredient in recipes or energy bars.

Does this all mean you should go out into your garden and eat earthworms? The answer is probably no. For a start, earthworms tend to taste of what they eat. Garden earthworms taste of soil, which is why food-grade earthworms are raised on a diet of vegetable scraps, cornmeal or other non-soil staples.

Did you know ?

The average energy content of an earthworm is 5 calories per gram. That makes your average Common earthworm (*Lumbricus terrestris*) about 20 calories or the same as two Brussels sprouts.

The second problem is that garden earthworms also contain potentially harmful parasites and bacteria so, unless you know what you're doing in terms of purging and cooking earthworms, you could end up being rather poorly. There have been a number of cases of people getting very sick from eating 'wild' earthworms, either on purpose or by accident. In one clinical case from the US, for example, a sixteen-year-old girl developed a cough, a number of blood disorders, and pulmonary disease one month after eating an earthworm as a dare.[15] Tests showed that the earthworm had been a carrier of *Toxocara* larvae, a disease-causing parasite that lives in the intestines of dogs and cats and can pass into their faeces and, ultimately, into the soil.

But perhaps, most importantly, the earthworm is a gardener's friend. Worms in the wild, as opposed to commercially farmed worms, perform such an important role in soil health that it seems counter-intuitive to start using them for food in the name of sustainability. It'd be like nibbling on a robin.

WHY DO SOME PEOPLE THINK EARTHWORMS ARE DISGUSTING?

EDIBLE, adj. Good to eat, and wholesome to digest, as a worm to a toad, a toad to a snake, a snake to a pig, a pig to a man, and a man to a worm.

Ambrose Bierce, from '*The Devil's Dictionary*'
in *The Collected Works of Ambrose Bierce* (1911)

Many people simply can't stomach the idea of eating annelids. Earthworm snacks are going to be a hard sell. But why should this be? During the 1990s, the London School of Tropical Medicine conducted an ambitious international survey to try to establish whether there were things that people – regardless of nationality or culture – found disgusting. While there were lots of cultural peculiarities and regional idiosyncrasies, there seemed to be a number of core things that most people, across the world, found repulsive. These were, in no particular order, bodily secretions, body parts (wounds, corpses, toenail clippings etc), decaying food, sick people and, curiously, worms.

Psychologists believe that, because the notion of worms being disgusting is so near-universal, it must have some genetic or evolutionary basis. We may have evolved to recoil from worms as a way of avoiding certain species that do us harm, especially human gut parasites such as tapeworms. Disgust for worms may therefore be hard-wired in our brains, even though most worms are harmless. For some people, the reaction is mild – only the idea of eating earthworms is challenging – while for others, even looking at an earthworm triggers their disgust response. Small-scale societies who do eat worms may have had to overcome their initial disgust response through necessity – as time has gone on, powerful and lasting cultural values have overlaid evolutionary ones.

EARTHWORM 'CURES'

And therefore, sir, as you desire to live, A day or two before your laxative, Take just three worms, nor under nor above, Because the gods unequal numbers love.

John Dryden, *'The Cock and the Fox'* (1700)

Earthworms have also been an ingredient in medicines for centuries. Folk doctors in Burma and India have long used earthworms in the treatment of various illnesses, including gum disease, post-partum weakness and smallpox.[16] In Iran, earthworms were baked into bread as a treatment for bladder stones, dried and eaten for jaundice, and their ashes rubbed into the scalp to encourage hair growth. In Chinese traditional medicine's *Compendium of Materia Medica*, written in the sixteenth century, the earthworm is described as the 'earth-dragon' and also prescribed as a remedy for jaundice, as well as being used as a diuretic and means of reducing fever. It's still used in China as a traditional remedy for convulsions and asthma.

The ancient Roman author and naturalist Pliny the Elder recommended earthworms as a cure for dozens of ailments in his treatise *Natural History*. In Book XXX, Chapter 39, 'Remedies Derived from Living Creatures', he helpfully suggests the following:

> Earthworms are so remarkably healing for wounds recently inflicted, that it is a very general belief that by the end of seven days they will unite sinews even that have been cut asunder: hence it is that it is recommended to keep them preserved in honey. Ashes of

burnt earthworms, in combination with tar or Simblian honey, cauterise the indurated margins of ulcerous sores. Some persons dry earthworms in the sun, and apply them to wounds with vinegar, the application not being removed till the end of a couple of days.

He also recommends burnt earthworms for the extraction of splintered bones, earthworms in raisin wine to expel a woman's afterbirth, earthworms rubbed on breast abscesses, and earthworms taken in honey wine to promote lactation. Earthworms boiled in oil and injected into the ear could offer – he suggested – relief from toothache or, rubbed on rotten teeth, burnt earthworms could make them come out more easily. The humble earthworm could even, continues Pliny, remove corns from the feet, prevent varicose veins, cure kidney stones, combat jaundice, treat cellulitis and stop your hair turning white.

Earthworms also found themselves in cures for animal ailments. One Yorkshire cure for horse distemper, for example, which appears in a 1764 edition of *The Scots Magazine*, includes a teacup full of earthworms tied up in a rag and boiled in ale.

While boil-in-the-bag earthworms aren't necessarily something to sample, the medical potential of the earthworm is just starting to be explored. Clinical studies have revealed that earthworms' bodies contain remarkable antibacterial, antioxidative, wound-healing, anti-inflammatory, anti-tumour, liver-protecting and anti-coagulative properties.[17] Such a rich range of biologically active components makes earthworms a potentially valuable source of medical treatments for the pharmaceutical industry. Problems such as cardiac or vascular diseases may, in the not too distant future, be treated with earthworm preparations. Apart from the hair restorer, looks like Pliny wasn't too far off.

Did you know

Not everyone thought earthworms could be medicinal. In 1908, a Buffalo physician, Dr Hiram Walker, was convinced that cancer was caused by earthworms. After seven years of research, he concluded that cancer was the result of parasites that oozed out of earthworms and recommended that his patients avoid contracting the disease by giving up all vegetables.

(Source: *The Dread Disease* by J.T. Patterson, 2009)

START A COMPOST HEAP

• Think of making compost like a recipe. Too much of one thing and the recipe won't work, but get the ingredients balanced and it'll give you dark, rich organic material to spread on your garden and encourage earthworms.

• There are two things a compost heap needs – nitrogen-rich ingredients and carbon-rich ingredients. Nitrogen-rich materials are usually lush, green or wet, like grass clippings, green leaves or vegetable peelings.

• Carbon-rich materials are usually drier and brown, such as cardboard or woody stems, and keep the compost nicely aerated. The ratio of green to brown ingredients should be 50:50, so for every armful of green material you'll need to add the same amount of brown material.

• You can make a compost heap in a pile, in a system of bays or boxes, or in a composting bin, whichever works for your size of garden and how much space you can dedicate to the compost area.

• Simply add layers of green and brown material throughout the year. Stick to the 50:50 rule and you shouldn't end up with either a sloppy, smelly mess (too much green stuff) or a dry, crispy heap that will take years to decompose (too much brown material). The wider the mix of materials, the better – don't let just one or two ingredients dominate. Overleaf you'll find a list of materials that count as either green or brown.

• Most people like to turn their compost regularly – i.e. once a month – to speed up decomposition. If you have an open compost heap, however, rather than a closed bin, you'll need to consider that there may be creatures such as hedgehogs, bumblebees and toads who are using the compost heap as a nesting site. In this instance, it's best to turn your compost just once a year, in late spring. This is the only time you can really dig around in your compost heap,

START A COMPOST HEAP (cont'd)

turning the contents over to aerate them, without the danger of injuring any animals who might be nesting in it. Hedgehogs, for example, hibernate in compost heaps between November and late March, but also use a compost heap as a nesting site or day nest between May and October. Some people choose not to turn their compost at all – this is fine, and you'll still end up with compost eventually, but it'll just take longer.

• Having a wormery in your garden can help improve the natural levels of earthworms in your soil. Wormeries are purpose-built containers that contain a colony of compost earthworms – usually Tiger worms (Eisena fetida) or similar. The earthworms live permanently in the wormery, turning your kitchen scraps and vegetable waste into nutritious compost and liquid fertiliser for the garden. Putting the wormery compost on your garden will then, in turn, attract more wild earthworms into the soil.

GREEN

- Grass clippings
- Raw vegetable and fruit waste/peelings
- Nettles
- Dead flowers
- Tea leaves
- Herbivore droppings e.g. horse/sheep manure (but never cat or dog faeces)
- Bird droppings
- Coffee grounds
- Pet/human hair

BROWN

- Shredded woody stems
- Prunings and hedge trimmings
- Wood/bark chippings
- Dead leaves
- Scrunched-up cardboard, brown paper, toilet roll tubes and egg boxes (crumpled up, these provide useful air pockets that help the decomposition process)
- Straw or hay
- Sawdust

The earthworm's body

I don't want to be a fly!

I want to be a worm!

Charlotte Perkins Gilman, '*A Conservative*' (1915)

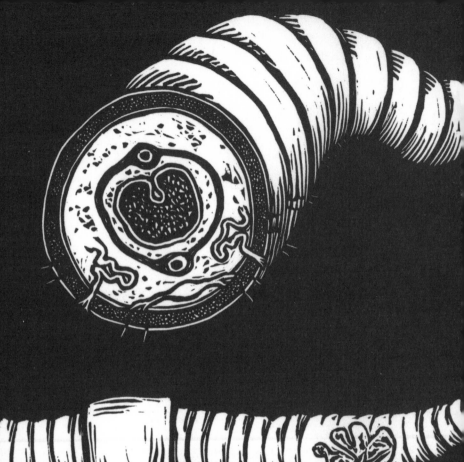
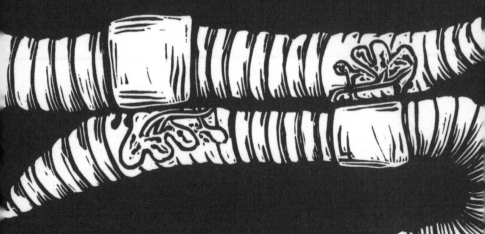

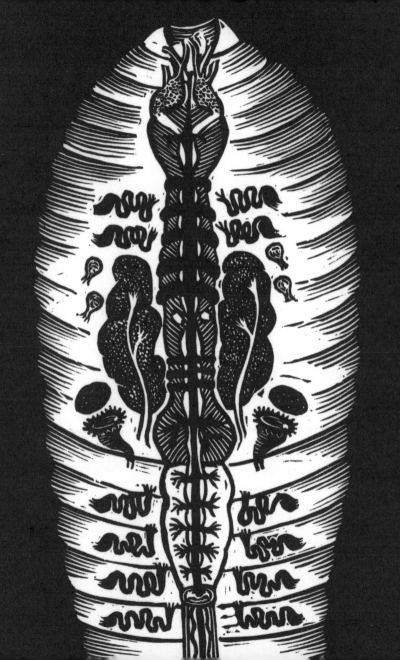

Earthworms are essentially one long digestive system with a mouth at one end and a bum at the other. They are invertebrates, which means they don't have a skeleton, so their bodies are made up of disc-like segments filled with muscles and fluid. Different species of earthworm have different numbers of segments – an adult Common earthworm (*Lumbricus terrestris*), for example, has between one hundred and one hundred and fifty segments.

DIGESTIVE SYSTEM – Earthworms are part of a group of segmented worms called Annelids (which means 'little rings') and are closely related to leeches and ragworms. Down the centre of each earthworm runs a digestive system – a mouth, followed by an oesophagus, crop (which stores food), gizzard (a kind of stomach that grinds food), intestine and finally the anus.

LUNGS AND HEART – Instead of having lungs, the earthworm breathes through its skin. It does this by having five pairs of simple 'hearts' called *aortic arches*, which sit near the head of the earthworm and pump blood around its body. When the blood flows close to its outer surface, it absorbs oxygen and releases carbon dioxide through a thin layer of skin. For this to happen, the earthworm's skin needs to be moist so, as well as living in damp conditions, the earthworm also coats itself in slime from its own mucus-secreting cells. If an earthworm dries out, it dies.

NERVOUS SYSTEM – Earthworms also have a brain and nervous system, which controls their movements and helps them detect environmental stimuli such as heat, chemical changes, vibrations, temperature and light. Their central nervous system consists of a simple brain and a long nerve cord, which runs almost the entire length of the earthworm's body. Along this nerve cord are little swellings, or *gangla*, in each individual segment. These small swellings act like mini-computers, each controlling its own segment. The nerve cord also has smaller nerves coming off it, which connect to the muscles and sensors of the worm, and together this system constantly 'reads' the earthworm's environment, helping it to move through the soil.

CAN EARTHWORMS SEE?

If you live underground, eyes aren't much use. That doesn't mean that earthworms can't 'see', or at least detect, light. Rather than a pair of eyes, like mammals, earthworms have cells – called *photoreceptors* – on their skin. These light-sensing cells can tell whether it's light or dark. This helps the earthworm know whether it's above or below ground and, if the earthworm needs to visit the surface, how bright the sunlight is.

Earthworms soon dry out and die if they're exposed to warm, sunny weather. Much of the activity of the Common earthworm (*Lumbricus terrestris*), for example, happens at night-time, away from the heat and light of the day. Under cover of darkness, they come to the surface to feed and mate, and can hopefully avoid predators (although many worm-devouring creatures, including hedgehogs, have also evolved to use this dusk-to-dawn window).

The earthworm's light receptors can also tell the difference between different coloured lights. They move away from white or blue light – the colours of daylight – but don't seem to react to red or orange lights, the colours of late-evening or early-morning light.

WHY DO EARTHWORMS SQUIRM IN DAYLIGHT?

...the earth without worms would soon become
cold, hardbound, and void of fermentation; and
consequently sterile...

Gilbert White, *The Natural History of Selborne* (1777)

arthworms are so sensitive to light that even just an
hour in daylight leaves them paralysed. In experiments that have looked into the effects of UV radiation on earthworms, scientists have found that different species have different tolerances. Unsurprisingly, surface dwellers typically can cope with more UV than deep or shallow burrowers. When exposed to light, however, no earthworm can cope indefinitely. Almost immediately, earthworms will start to have abnormally strong muscle contractions, often making those characteristic 'S'-shaped movements or seeming to jump and flick about – we don't know why they do this 'dance of death' but it may be something to do with UV light causing earthworms to become confused and poorly coordinated.[18] After only a short period, however, UV light starts to damage the earthworm's skin cells – the earthworm needs its skin to breathe and so, in effect, it suffocates

to death. That's ultimately why, come the morning's bright sunshine, an earthworm, as Darwin noted, 'dashes like a rabbit into its burrow'.

WHICH END OF AN EARTHWORM IS WHICH?

The easiest way to tell the head from the tail is to look for something called the *clitellum*. This is a fleshy ring around the worm, which is also called the 'saddle'. The clitellum is always nearer the head end.

Young earthworms don't have a clitellum. These only appear when the earthworm is sexually mature. So, if an earthworm has no saddle (and about 50 per cent of earthworms are juveniles), look which way the worm is travelling, as they tend to go head first. Earthworms can move backwards but usually only do it if their head touches something noxious.[19] If you look *really* closely at an earthworm, you might even be able to make out the *prostomium* on its head – a kind of shelf-like lip that covers its mouth.

HOW DO
EARTHWORMS MOVE?

Earthworms move along their burrows by contracting and expanding muscles. Each earthworm has two sets of muscles: the first set encircles each of their segments, like a body-length corset; the second set runs from head to tip, like a long rubber band. Contracting these sets of muscles, at different times, helps the earthworm move forwards.

When an earthworm wants to move in a forwards direction, it squeezes the circular muscles around each of its segments; contracting these corset-like muscles allows the earthworm to stretch out forwards and become longer and thinner.

Now the earthworm is stretched out to its fullest, it needs to pull the back end of its body forwards. To do this, it contracts the rubber-band-like muscles – which run lengthwise down its body (i.e. parallel to the earthworm's body) – making its body fatter and shorter again.

This constant stretching and pulling its body forwards, however, only works if the earthworm can somehow anchor itself in the soil. If it couldn't, the worm would constantly slip on the same spot. So, to anchor itself into the soil, the earthworm has a special trick – it has tiny retractable bristle-like structures called *setae* along its body, which it can push and pull – like climbers' crampons – out of the soil. Each segment of the worm has eight of these bristles.

So, to move forwards, one complete cycle of an earthworm stretch would go like this:

1. Contract the corset-like muscles to extend the body forwards.
2. Grip the soil with the setae at the front end of the body.
3. Contract the rubber-band-like muscles to 'pull' the back end of the worm forwards.
4. Grip the soil with the setae on the back end of the body and extend the body forwards again.

HOW STRONG IS
AN EARTHWORM?

To move through the earth, earthworms burrow by force-fully enlarging tiny crevices and cracks in the soil. This can take an enormous amount of pressure and strength – in experiments that have measured the force needed for an earthworm to tunnel its way through the ground, it was found that large adults could push ten times their own body weight. That's the equivalent of a human pushing a large polar bear or bison out of his or her way.

Did you know

What's even more extraordinary is that tiny hatchlings – baby earthworms – can push five hundred times their own body weight – that's the same as a person casually shoving a humpback whale to one side.

HOW FAST CAN AN
EARTHWORM TRAVEL?

A worm is as good a traveler as a grasshopper or a
cricket, and a much wiser settler.

Henry David Thoreau,
A Week on the Concord and Merrimack Rivers (1849)

The Common earthworm (*Lumbricus terrestris*) is generally a slow mover, meandering gently through the soil,
but the speed at which it travels depends on a number of factors, including the size of the worm, the structure of the soil
and why the earthworm is moving.

Few people have studied how fast earthworms travel.
However, one study, published in the *Journal of Experimental
Biology*, provides some interesting insights.[20] The first is
that, perhaps not surprisingly, larger earthworms can go
faster than smaller earthworms. To pick up pace, earthworms of all sizes seem to increase their stride length,
i.e. they stretch out further with each movement. Smaller
worms, however, also have a tendency to increase the frequency of their strides to go faster, while large worms take
fewer but comparatively longer strides.

LOVE LEAVES

- Fallen leaves have long been regarded by gardeners as something to be tidied away, to be scraped off the lawn, bagged up and thrown in the bin. Not only are we missing out on a free source of nutrients for our soil, we are removing a key habitat for a wide range of creatures who need leaf litter to survive.

- Dead and decaying leaves are a vital source of food and shelter for many invertebrates, especially over winter. The insulating effect of a carpet of leaves allows spiders, beetles, flies, snails and many other creatures to endure cold temperatures; some overwinter as eggs, others ride out the weather as larvae or cocoons, while many species survive in adult form, waiting for the return of spring by wrapping themselves up in leaves or snuggling below the blanket of litter. Larger animals also rely on piles of leaves – hedgehogs, mice

and other mammals use the leaves as bedding or nesting material – while garden birds love nothing more than searching for bugs among the debris.

• Any area of the garden that has a high density of leaf litter is also an absolute haven for surface-dwelling earthworms (epigeic earthworms). Plants that produce an abundance of falling leaves – hedges, deciduous trees, shrubs – will attract surface-dwelling earthworms in large numbers. If you can't leave the leaves where they fall, try and pile them somewhere else in the garden – you'll not only be creating a habitat for wildlife but, over time, you'll also end up with a rich source of leaf mould for your garden soil.

Using the data from the study – which measured earthworms ranging in size from a minuscule 0.2 grams to a healthy 8 grams – it has been calculated that the Common earthworm travels at the following speeds, depending on its relative size:

- Tiny earthworms can crawl about 12 centimetres per minute or 7.2 metres per hour.
- Medium-sized earthworms can crawl about 90 centimetres per minute or 54 metres per hour.
- Large earthworms can crawl about 1.2 metres per minute or 72 metres per hour.

In effect, larger Common earthworms can travel ten times faster than the smaller ones. Whether earthworms do actually travel at these speeds consistently when they're underground, we don't know. The texture and composition of the soil, for instance, radically affects how fast earthworms can burrow – it can take deep-burrowing worms four or five times longer to move through clay than light loam.

What we do know, however, is that earthworms can move *really* fast if they want to. Earthworms have superfast nerve impulses, which can race down the entire length of their body at speeds as high as 600 metres per second. Touch an earthworm when it's poking its head out of the soil and it'll retreat, quick as a flash.

DO WORMS HAVE TASTE BUDS?

The short answer is no. Earthworms don't have a tongue, so they don't have taste buds. However, they do have a sense of taste and smell – it's just different from ours.

In earthworms, the same receptors serve for the senses of taste and smell. They're called *chemoreceptors* and can detect different chemical stimuli. Experiments have shown that earthworms have these special receptors inside their mouths and on their *prostomium* – a firm lip-like projection over their mouths that they use to push their way through the soil. They use these receptors to seek out and choose food, to sense how much water there is in the soil, and to find other worms to mate with.

Darwin spent a great deal of time trying to establish whether the Common earthworm (*Lumbricus terrestris*) had any food preferences. Of the foods he offered to his subterranean 'dinner guests', he concluded that 'Cabbage-leaves are much liked by worms; and it appears that they can distinguish between different varieties' and that carrots, onion leaves, wild cherry leaves and celery were particular favourites. His conclusions were startling, not because Darwin established the menu of choice of earthworms (he only offered a limited range of food options) but because he proved earthworms were making definite selections of one food type over another (see *What Do Earthworms Eat?* page 98).

CAN EARTHWORMS SURVIVE UNDERWATER?

'…there are many arguments which tend to show that these purely land-dwellers have grown out of exclusively water-dwellers… For there are here and there vestiges of structures which seem only fitted for an aquatic life…'

Frank E. Beddard, *Earthworms and their Allies* (1912)

In 1874, a scientist called Edmond Perrier tested how long Common earthworms (*Lumbricus terrestris*) could survive submerged in tap water. To his surprise, if the water was frequently changed, the worms lasted for more than

four months. Similar results have been reported for a number of other earthworm species.

What's interesting is that, although earthworms have become an important land animal, they originally evolved in the ocean. Most annelids, the family to which earthworms belong, still live in wet environments, whether it's oceans, fresh water or damp soil. In fact, many species of earthworm are so adept at surviving in waterlogged conditions or aerated water that earthworms used in water submersion experiments usually died of starvation rather than 'drowning'.

When you see dead or dying earthworms on the ground surface after a heavy rainstorm, this is not because they have drowned, but more likely because of exposure to daylight (see *Why do earthworms surface after rain?* page 88).

WHY ARE EARTHWORMS SLIMY?

Earthworms secrete 'slime' or mucus for a number of reasons: the first is so they can breathe through their skin. Rather than use lungs to breathe, earthworms diffuse oxygen and carbon dioxide through their skin and for this to happen the surface has to be moist.

They also coat themselves in mucus to help them move more easily through soil. A recent study showed that earthworm mucus is incredibly effective at stopping soil particles sticking to their bodies. This sliminess reduces drag as the earthworm travels through the soil, making its movements quicker and more agile. In fact, earthworm mucus is so efficient at this process that researchers are looking into how they can apply this lubricating quality to farmers' soil-tillage implements, which often struggle when soil sticks to their surface.[21]

Earthworms also produce lots of mucus during sex. When two earthworms are ready to reproduce, they cover themselves in a layer of slime so they can stick together and swap sperm (see *How do earthworms have sex?* page 113). Deep-burrowing species, such as the Common earthworm

(*Lumbricus terrestris*), also use mucus to cement the walls of their burrows to stop the tunnels from collapsing.

In-depth studies of one exotic species – the large New Zealand earthworm (*Octochaetus multiporus*) – suggest that we're only just beginning to understand what a powerful substance earthworm slime is. Scientist Anna Palmer, who has been studying earthworms since she was a child, investigated the mucus of the *Octochaetus multiporus* and found a number of remarkable qualities: the first was that the mucus was extremely toxic to soil bacteria, keeping the earthworm's body relatively free from disease. The second was that the mucus contained trace elements of thirty-three metals and minerals, including magnesium, potassium and calcium. These last three elements are vital for healthy plant growth and may explain, in part, why plants grown in earthworm-rich soil do so much better than in worm-free ground.

The *Octochaetus multiporus* earthworm also has another trick up its sleeve – bioluminescent slime. Its glow-in-the-dark mucus indicates the age of the earthworm as it matures, changing from blue to yellowy-orange over the course of its life. *Octochaetus multiporus* also squirts out bioluminescent fluid when it is accidentally disturbed.

It's not clear why these earthworms, and a small number of other species of worm, have this glow-in-the-dark function. Depending on how it is deployed, it may be a lure or a deterrent. Gentle, glowing bioluminescence can be a way of attracting a potential mate – the changing colour of the *Octochaetus multiporus* slime may signal sexual maturity to another eager worm. But fast-response, sudden squirts of their glow-in-the-dark slime might be used, instead, as an effective deterrent against predators. Whether its purpose is to startle and confuse a potential attacker, or warn a predator of its toxicity, we still don't know.[22]

Mucus is also the latest ingredient to be harnessed by the beauty industry. Earthworm slime – which is thought to contain useful peptides and enzymes – is washed from worm casts and extracted by submerging earthworms in water, and then added to anti-wrinkle and skin regeneration creams.

CAN EARTHWORMS HEAR?

Disdain thee! – not the worm beneath my feet!

Percy Shelley, *Hellas* (1822)

Earthworms don't have ears but they are very sensitive to vibrations caused by sound. One of the loveliest images conjured up by Darwin during his observations involved him playing a number of musical instruments to his earthworm subjects.

Despite his best efforts, 'They took not the least notice of the shrill notes from a metal whistle, which was repeatedly sounded near them; nor did they of the deepest and loudest tones of a bassoon. They were indifferent to shouts, if care was taken that the breath did not strike them. When placed on a table close to the keys of a piano, which was played as loudly as possible, they remained perfectly quiet.'

The earthworms did react, however, when they were placed on the piano in pots of soil. 'When the note C in the bass clef was struck, both instantly retreated into their burrows. After a time they emerged, and when

G above the line in the treble clef was struck, they again retreated.' Darwin concluded that, although earthworms aren't bothered by loud noises, they are very sensitive to sound vibrations (see *Why do earthworms surface after rain?* page 88).

CAN AN EARTHWORM REGROW IF IT'S CUT IN HALF?

One of the most common myths about earthworms is that if you cut one in half, both halves survive to become two new worms.

Whether an earthworm will survive being chopped in two depends on where it's cut. The Common earthworm (*Lumbricus terrestris*) will generally survive having a bit of its tail end cut off and can even regrow some of its segments, creating a new tail. The old, chopped tail end will die. Chop an earthworm anywhere at the front end between its saddle (*clitellum*) and its head, however, and you'll kill it stone dead, as this is where its major organs are.

Some species of earthworms are better at coping with being chopped in two than others, but all seem to have the capacity to regrow at least some segments of their tails. In fact, some species of earthworms can deliberately detach or self-amputate their tail if they have been caught by a predator, in a behaviour called *autotomy* (some species of reptiles do the same). Sometimes an earthworm will detach its own tail for different reasons: the compost earthworm *Eisenia fetida*, for example, uses the end of its own tail as a kind of refuse dump for insoluble waste, which gives it a characteristic yellow colour. When the worm can't store any more waste in that section of the tail, like a spent rocket-ship it simply jettisons the tip.

One worm can regenerate almost endlessly, however. Planarians are simple flatworms. They're only loosely related to earthworms but have been shown to have spectacular regenerative powers. Cut a planarian up into pieces and each piece will grow into a completely new worm. In one experiment, a piece of planarian that was only 1/279th of the original worm regrew into an entirely new clone of itself. That's like an entire person regrowing from a piece of human tissue the size of a hamster.[*]

---

[*] Calculation based on average human weight of 62 kg and an adult hamster weighing just over 200 g.

Did you know ?

In 2015, thousands of earthworms rained from the skies over southern Norway. Freak weather events, such as water-spouts and tornados, are thought to pick up vegetation and small animals and carry them for miles before dropping them again.
A similar event happened in 2011 at a Selkirkshire school in Scotland, when a teacher and his students had to take cover during a football game after earthworms began plummeting from the sky.

Earthworm behaviour

But it is surprising that an animal
so low in the scale as a worm should have
the capacity for acting in this manner

Charles Darwin, *The Formation of Vegetable Mould
through the Action of Worms, with Observations
on their Habits* (1881)

What does an earthworm do all day? Darwin was one of the first scientists to document, with any rigour, the idiosyncrasies of earthworms. Since then, subsequent studies and experiments have revealed some extraordinary behaviours. From 'herding' instincts to weather preferences, courtship rituals to defensive mechanisms, there's much more to the average earthworm than meets the eye.

Other questions, such as do earthworms sleep, can they feel pain, or how do they find a mate, are still being explored – it seems there's still plenty we don't fully understand about life underground.

WHY DO EARTHWORMS SURFACE AFTER RAIN?

> The next time you go out on your morning or evening ramble, if you chance to see a worm in your path, do not kick it aside, not step over it; but take it from the ground, and lay it in the palm of your hand...

James Samuelson, *Humble Creatures* (1858)

Have you ever noticed that earthworms tend to head to the surface after a rainstorm? Scientists used to think that worms headed upwards through the soil to prevent them drowning in their water-filled burrows. We now suspect this isn't true, as earthworms prefer moist soil and many species can actually survive submerged in oxygen-rich water for weeks (see *Can earthworms survive underwater?* page 74).

We still don't know for certain why earthworms head upwards during a rainstorm, but one theory is that it might be something to do with migration and that earthworms find it easier to move bigger distances across the wet soil surface than going through the soil, especially if it's dry.

It's a risky strategy, however, as exposure to strong UV light can be lethal for an earthworm, so another more convincing theory is that the drumming of the rain mimics the vibrations of moles digging through the soil. In order to avoid being eaten, on hearing these vibrations earthworms move up through the soil to get out of the way. Certain species of birds, including seagulls, blackbirds and thrushes, actually mimic this vibration by tapping the ground with their feet to lure unsuspecting earthworms to the surface, where they are gobbled up. Worm charmers use the same trick.

Scientists recently tested this hypothesis. At the Annual Sopchoppy Worm Gruntin' Festival in Florida, worm charmers use a special trick to entice earthworms to the surface. They hammer wooden stakes about 30 centimetres into the soil and then scrape the stake with a long piece of steel called a 'rooping iron'. The rhythmic, rasping noises that are created by steel scraping on the wood sound like low-pitched grunts (hence the name for the festival) and without fail seem to bring hundreds of earthworms to the surface.

The researchers wanted to explain why the 'rooping' technique worked and set up seismic recording equipment to measure what was happening underground. It turned out that scraping with a rooping iron caused vibrations that registered about 100 hertz, an almost identical frequency to the sound of moles digging. The flight response of earthworms to the sound of moles is thought to be an evolutionary one, and deep-seated. In countries such as New Zealand, which don't even have moles, earthworms seem to have a 'memory' of this predator and still behave in the same way if they hear vibrations.

Did you know ?

On 14 September 1972, Cleveland Airport was brought to a standstill when hundreds of thousands of earthworms appeared on the runway. Heavy rain had brought the worms to the surface of the ground and they'd inadvertently crawled on to the runway, causing aircraft to skid dangerously on landing.

WHY IS IT DIFFICULT TO PULL AN EARTHWORM OUT OF A HOLE?

It's surprisingly difficult to pull an earthworm back out of the soil if it's burrowing. Writing in the middle of the nineteenth century, the nature writer James Samuelson noted: 'It has perhaps never occurred to you to enquire how it is, when you endeavour to draw a worm forth from the earth, that it can offer such resistance to your efforts, as almost to necessitate your tearing it in two before you can extract it.'[23] Darwin also noticed that they 'can seldom be dragged out of the ground without being torn to pieces' and we can often observe garden birds struggling to winkle them out of the soil.

We already know that the earthworm's body is actually covered in tiny stiff bristles called setae (see *How do earthworms move?* page 66). These setae face slightly backwards,

GROW GREEN 'MANURES'

Research has shown that using cover crops is an easy way to introduce organic material to the soil and boost earthworm numbers by as much as 300 per cent.[25]

• Plant a cover crop in a vegetable garden at the end of summer. Also known as 'green manures', cover crops protect the otherwise bare soil over autumn and winter, reducing the amount of weeds and preventing the soil from becoming too cold. At the end of the winter season, cover crops are dug back into the soil,

organically nourishing the earth and helping feed the plants that follow – for winter cover crops, look for plants such as grazing rye or winter vetch.

• You can also use cover crops during the growing season to 'fill in' spaces where you have lifted out your other vegetables and to attract pollinating insects – mustard, crimson clover and phacelia are lightning quick to germinate and will grow in just a few weeks.

helping the earthworm anchor itself into the ground as it pushes itself forwards through the soil. Without them, the earthworm would just slide around on the same spot. These little spikes also make it difficult to pull an earthworm out of its burrow, especially tail first, as the bristles dig in and create resistance. If a garden bird grabs a worm by its front end, it probably has a better chance of pulling it out of its burrow. In the struggle, the earthworm's setae can fall off. If the worm manages to escape and live to tell the tale, its bristles will grow back, just like fingernails.

Experiments also suggest that garden birds, such as robins, carefully listen for cues that an earthworm is close by. Once the sound of an earthworm is located, some garden birds cock their heads to one side. We used to think this was so they could listen even more closely, but recent research suggests garden birds are head-cocking to locate the earthworm by sight, before they make their final, deadly strike.[24]

DO EARTHWORMS LIKE WARM OR COLD WEATHER?

We do not avoid evil by fleeing before it,
but by rising above or diving below its plane;
as the worm escapes drought and frost by
boring a few inches deeper.

Henry David Thoreau,
A Week on the Concord and Merrimack Rivers (1849)

Earthworms are at the whim of the weather. Unlike mammals, which can regulate their own body temperature, the earthworm is a cold-blooded creature and its temperature is directly affected by its surroundings.

Different species of earthworms, however, prefer different temperatures. Surface dwellers, such as the composter's favourite – the Tiger worm (*Eisenia fetida*) – can tolerate temperatures between 0°C and 35°C but seem happiest at a balmy 25°C. The Common earthworm (*Lumbricus terrestris*), on the other hand, prefers life deep in the soil, where it's a cooler and more consistent temperature throughout the year.

Deep soil temperature is remarkably stable.

At the surface and just under, the soil temperature rises and falls in line with changes in the surrounding air temperature. The further down into the soil you go, however, the less the soil is affected by the temperature of the air. At 4 metres underground, the soil temperature is a fairly steady 10°C, at 1.5 metres underground it varies between about 5°C and 15°C, and at 50 centimetres underground, the temperature can fluctuate between just above freezing and just under 20°C.

Given that the Common earthworm's optimum temperature is between 7°C and 12°C, it makes sense for the earthworm to move around in the soil, searching for the most comfortable temperatures. In winter, this means spending much of its time in the deeper layers of soil. The Common earthworm can't tolerate temperatures below freezing but their egg cocoons can survive for weeks in soil as cold as –5°C. Each cocoon has a protective dehydration mechanism; in response to sub-zero temperatures, the cocoon begins to lose water, effectively freeze-drying itself until conditions improve and the weather warms up.

Other species of earthworm, including Nordenskiold's worm (*Eisenia nordenskioldi*), found across large parts of Russia, and the Octagonal-tailed worm (*Dendrobaena octaedra*), native to Eastern Europe and Western Siberia, have to cope with long, very harsh winters. They have evolved a neat trick whereby they rapidly increase the amount of glucose in their body fluids, which acts like a natural antifreeze and stops their bodies being destroyed by ice crystals.

Back in temperate climates, if soil becomes too hot or too dry, some species – including the Common earthworm – will go into a period of dormancy called *aestivation*. The main aim of aestivation is to stay moist, so the earthworm coils itself into a tight knot to reduce its surface area, seals itself in a chamber lined with mucus to keep the humidity high, and lowers its metabolism so it doesn't lose too much water. Then, in this 'summer stasis', the earthworm can sit out the scorching temperatures and dry soil for as long as three weeks, until things return to normal.

WHAT DO EARTHWORMS EAT?

It depends on the species of earthworm. Surface dwellers eat decaying organic matter – such as dead leaves, berries, rotting wood and flowers. Shallow-dwelling earthworms eat soil, which is high in organic matter. And deep-burrowing earthworms drag larger pieces of decaying plant material, such as leaves, into their burrows. Some species of earthworm also eat fungus and rotting animals.

Did you know

People sometimes call earthworms 'omnivores', but a more accurate term is a 'detritivore' or animal that feeds on dead organic material.

One of the mysteries of earthworm eating habits was how they coped with toxic plants. Some plants are spectacularly poisonous and contain chemicals – called polyphenols – designed to stop them being stripped by herbivores. These toxins still carry on being potent even after the plant or its leaves are dead.

Scientists at Imperial College, however, worked out how earthworms seem to be able to stomach almost anything, even if it's poisonous. It turns out that earthworms' guts contain molecules – called *drilodefensins* – that neutralise certain chemicals. No other animal on the planet has these toxin-busting molecules – drilodefensins are found only in the guts of earthworms.[26]

What's really interesting about earthworms, however, is what comes out of their back ends. Worm poo or 'worm casts' are wonderfully rich in nutrients and minerals, which are in a form readily available for plants to use. Compared to the surrounding soil, worm casts contain on average five times more nitrogen, seven times more phosphorus and eleven times more potassium.[27]

The constant eating and pooing of earthworms moves an extraordinary amount of soil. Worm casts deposited on the soil surface slowly accumulate, burying whatever is lying on the surface – this is often how archaeological artefacts and ancient monuments get slowly submerged over centuries. It's estimated that in just one single acre of land, earthworms add a fresh, 5-centimetre layer of topsoil every year. That's about 8 tons of soil.

DO EARTHWORMS BUILD HOMES UNDERGROUND?

The very name Earthworm, so distinctive as
it is of the habitat of these animals, seems
to have been expressly invented in order
to crystallise into one word the remarkable
distributions of these creatures.

Frank E. Beddard, *Earthworms and their Allies* (1912)

Most earthworms don't have homes. Both surface dwellers and shallow-dwelling species move through organic matter, eating and pooing it out behind them in the form of crumbly worm casts.

Surface dwellers don't create burrows at all – they don't live in the soil – and prefer life under layers of moist, warm leaf litter. Shallow-dwelling species do create tunnels as they eat their way through the soil but quickly fill them up again with excreted worm casts as they move along.

Deep-burrowing species, however, such as the Common earthworm (*Lumbricus terrestris*) create permanent burrows, which they keep clear of debris. To do this, they leave their poo on the surface of the soil, at the entrance to their burrow, in piles known as 'middens'. Unless it's disturbed, the earthworm will stay in the same burrow its whole life and keep adding to the midden, creating an ever-increasing pile of poo. These permanent burrows are so well constructed they can remain stable for decades.

Darwin noted that his Common earthworms sometimes even built little roofs over their burrows: 'Where fallen leaves are abundant, many more are sometimes collected over the mouth of a burrow than can be used, so that a small pile of unused leaves is left like a roof over those which have been partly dragged in... They often or generally fill up the interstices between the drawn-in leaves with moist viscid earth ejected from their bodies, and thus the mouths of the burrows are securely plugged.' Why they did this, Darwin wasn't sure, but he suspected the leaves provided a means of regulating temperature and humidity within the burrows, acted as rain covers, and offered a level of concealment from hungry predators.

ARE EARTHWORMS TERRITORIAL?

While surface-dwellers and shallow-burrowing species of earthworm don't have permanent burrows, there's no place like home for the Common earthworm (*Lumbricus terrestris*).

When the Common earthworm comes out at night – to search for food and find a mate – it will try to cling on to the top of its burrow with the tip of its tail. This not only helps the earthworm make a speedy exit should it get attacked by a predator but it also prevents the earthworm from losing its way home. Common earthworms do, however, sometimes venture further afield, leaving the safety of their burrows. Tests have shown that they have a homing instinct – in one study, Common earthworms found their way home after more than three hours on the soil surface and from as far away as nearly a metre. To return to base, the earthworm carefully backed along its own outward trail until its tail reached the top of the burrow.[28]

It's thought that Common earthworms also leave a chemical trail that contains pheromones. Serving as a guidance system back to the burrow, the trail acts as an 'attractant', encouraging the earthworm to follow its own scent until it reaches home. Other species, such as the American River worm (*Diplocardia riparia*), leave a 'repellent' pheromone trail, which the worm actively avoids trying to come into contact with again. This species of worm is a scavenger and, as such, doesn't need to find its way home or want to follow the same trail twice looking for food.

Common earthworms may even 'pass on' their burrows to their offspring after death. The earthworm lays its cocoon in its burrow – usually in the topsoil layer – either partly embedded in the burrow wall or placed on a tiny 'nursery' side burrow, dug horizontally from the vertical shaft (cocoons can survive much colder temperatures than adult earthworms – see *Do Worms like cold or warm weather?* page 95). Researchers have observed juvenile earthworms taking up residence in burrows abandoned by an adult earthworm when it dies. The large amount of energy it takes to build a burrow may be one of the reasons why a juvenile could 'inherit' the family home, although adult earthworms don't share a burrow and most young earthworms have to make their own way as soon as they are big enough.

WHAT ANIMALS EAT EARTHWORMS?

The earthworm is possibly the favourite thing on a mole's menu. A typical European mole (*Talpa europaea*) can eat sixty earthworms in a day. Rather than 'hunting' through the soil, which would be an exhausting, hit-and-miss process, the mole has developed a number of canny strategies to ensure his or her fill of earthworms.

The first is that mole tunnels are effective and deadly 'earthworm traps'. Moles are surprisingly fast movers – if they hear a worm inadvertently stumbling into one of their tunnels, they race along and grab the worm before it has chance to escape.

During summer, however, deep-burrowing earthworm activity slows down – many just head deeper down into the soil and go into a period of dormancy called *aestivation* (see *Do earthworms like warm or cold weather?* page 95). This means earthworms are less likely to come into contact with mole burrows. As a way of surviving these leaner months, moles create 'larders' where they keep earthworms to eat later. Mole saliva contains a toxin that paralyses the earthworm but keeps it alive; one quick chomp to the head and the worm is immobilised but can be kept fresh for weeks.

Moles have been known to keep hundreds of 'zombie' worms in these special storage chambers, in a kind of hellish stasis – alive but unable to wriggle away.

When the time finally comes to eat the earthworm, the mole has one last trick up its sleeve. To maximise the nutrition from the worm, the mole doesn't want to eat all the soil that is sitting in the earthworm's gut. So, in the same way you squeeze toothpaste from a tube, the mole pushes the earthworm between its paws to remove all the earth and dirt from its body. This purging of soil from the earthworm may also help to minimise the amount of wear and tear on the mole's teeth, which would otherwise be quickly worn down from the abrasive effects of chomping through endless gritty material.

Earthworms are the staple diet of many other mammals, including hedgehogs, badgers, shrews, weasels, otters and stoats. Many of the species that feed on earthworms are nocturnal and take advantage of the feeding habits and lengthy night-time mating rituals of certain earthworm species. Foxes and owls, for example, are well known for foraging on juicy, large Common earthworms (*Lumbricus terrestris*) when they surface under the cover of darkness.

Many birds eat earthworms. In parks and suburbs, common garden birds such as blackbirds, thrushes and robins feed voraciously on earthworms; on farmland, it's starlings, rooks, lapwings and gulls that often follow the plough or harrow as it disturbs the soil. You may sometimes have wondered why it is that seagulls – whose natural habitat is by the seaside – are so good at locating farmers ploughing up their soil miles inland. The answer may be that gulls spend much of their time at very high altitudes and have super-keen eyesight.

Did you know

The eastern Australian duck-billed platypus is also rather partial to earthworms and can eat 800 in a single day. They are one of the only animals who find their food by *electrolocation.* As the platypus pushes its bill through the mud in the bottom of streams and rivers, its electroreceptors pick up minute electrical currents generated by the earthworm's muscular contractions.

At such great heights they can survey land for many miles around, which helps them locate feeding opportunities. Gulls also keep an eye out for lapwings; lapwings live on farmland and soon gather behind a tractor if it's churning through soil. The presence of a group of lapwings tells the gulls, who are high above, that there's a feast of earthworms and other invertebrates below. Gulls feeding at ground level then attract other gulls and so, in no time at all, you have a huge flock of birds swooping and diving behind a tractor, hoping for a juicy worm or two.

Different birds feed on different species of earthworm, depending on their foraging strategy; robins, which rely on visual or auditory cues, tend to eat surface dwellers or deep-burrowing earthworms when they come up to the top of their tunnels, while long-billed sandpipers, which use their beaks to probe the soil and search for earthworms by touch, tend to hunt for shallow-dwelling earthworms that live just under the surface. Certain species of birds, such as lapwings, gulls, plovers, thrushes and blackbirds, also 'paddle' for worms. They stamp the surface of the ground with their feet to mimic the sound of vibrations caused by burrowing moles, sending the worms underground fleeing to the surface.

A number of other insects also eat earthworms, although some prefer their meals less wriggly than others. It's not a subject well studied and the few examples we have often come from amateur sightings or surprise moments captured in the process of filming wildlife documentaries. In a lovely letter published in the *Monthly Review* in the early part of the nineteenth century, the editor notes: 'A letter to the Secretary from Mr. Power of Market Bosworth, Leicestershire, was read, describing the manner in which the common garden snail... and the slug... feed on the common dew worm or earth worm *Lumbricus terrestris*, when dead or dying. This is performed in the night; and as Mr Power observed these animals would not attack a living worm, he attributes it to the prickles on its surface, which the worm, when in health and vigour, has a power of erecting, as well probably for defence against snails, as for the purpose of drawing straws, &c. into its retreat.'[29]

One remarkable animal that preys on earthworms looks rather like a giant earthworm itself. The caecilian is a limbless, snake-like amphibian that can be found in the tropical regions of South and Central America, Africa and southern Asia. It has incredibly powerful jaws and scientists long wondered why an animal that preferred its meals in the form of soft and juicy earthworms needed such a strong bite. Researchers watched how caecilians ate their worms and, to their astonishment, observed them spinning vigorously like a crocodile's 'death roll' in an attempt to rip the earthworm into tiny pieces. When the bits digested earthworm were recovered from a caecilian, each fragment looked like twisted rope. This amazing strategy explains the bite strength – only by having such powerful jaws can the caecilian grip on to the earthworm as it corkscrews. By tearing the earthworm into small chunks, the caecilian can devour its prey without any grasping limbs.[30]

WATER THE WORMS

• Worms thrive
in a cool, damp
environment. Adding a
decent layer of organic
material to your soil (see
*How to help earthworms
#1* page 28) will help
keep moisture trapped
in the soil but it's also
important to water your
garden or allotment over
the warmer months if
the soil gets too dry.

• Always water in the
early morning, when the
weather is still cool, or
the early evening.
This not only stops
too much of the water
being evaporated by
the heat of the day but
also prevents pollinating
insects such as bees and
butterflies from feeling
the full force of
a hosepipe.

CAN EARTHWORMS
DEFEND THEMSELVES?

I sometimes think we consider too much the good
luck of the early bird and not enough the bad luck
of the early worm.

Franklin D. Roosevelt to Henry M. Heymann (1919)

Despite their soft, vulnerable bodies, earthworms have a few strategies to give themselves a fighting chance when predators attack. Many species, including the Common earthworm (*Lumbricus terrestris*), will, if grabbed, thrash about wildly in an effort to free themselves. If the earthworm's tail is ripped off in the fight, it may grow another one back (see *Can an earthworm regrow if it's cut in half?* page 80). As we have seen, some species of earthworms, including the Grey worm (*Aporrectodea caliginosa*), deliberately drop their tails as a defence mechanism, a practice known as *autotomy* (see page 81).

Some species of earthworm secrete a noxious fluid if they are under threat. Australia has at least two 'shooters' – the Giant Gippsland worm (*Megascolides australis*) can fire fluid up to 10 centimetres away from its body, while *Didymogaster sylvaticus* can reach three times that distance, earning itself the rather brilliant nickname 'Squirter worm'. Even the well-known Tiger worm, found in many a compost bin, emits a disgusting, rotted-garlic-like liquid if it's distressed or roughly handled – the second part of its Latin name, *Eisenia fetida*, literally means 'foul-smelling'.

Some scientists also suspect that the earthworms' own bristles, or setae, make them unpalatable to some other insects. We know, for example, that earthworms have setae sharp enough to pierce another earthworm's skin during mating (see *How do earthworms have sex?* page 113), so perhaps these bristles are also enough to make certain insects think twice before attacking.

HOW DO EARTHWORMS HAVE SEX?

There are no male or female earthworms – they're hermaphrodites, which means each earthworm has both male and female sexual parts.

For an earthworm to reproduce, it has to be sexually mature. This only occurs once that characteristic 'saddle' or clitellum appears on the earthworm's body; on the Common earthworm (*Lumbricus terrestris*), the clitellum appears at about six weeks old and sits about a third of the way down its body, nearest the head end.

Earthworms also select similar-sized partners, probably because it would make for tricky sex to be wildly different in size. Age doesn't seem to come into it, however, and studies have shown that old earthworms can successfully inseminate young ones. In an interesting study of Tiger worms (*Eisenia fetida*),[31] it was found that sperm production didn't really decrease with age, even when the worm was six years old. The same worm's female reproductive functions, however, dropped off radically after three years. An old earthworm, therefore, can get another earthworm pregnant, but may struggle to be itself impregnated.

The courtship ritual of the Common earthworm is a tender affair, with an initial 'getting to know you' session that involves prospective partners visiting each other's burrows above ground. Under the cover of darkness, an earthworm will stretch out and attempt to poke its head into a neighbouring burrow, keeping the tip of its own tail anchored in its own burrow should it need to make a hasty retreat. The number of times an earthworm visits a mate's burrow varies – sometimes only once or twice, at other times more than a dozen. The visits are often brief, 30–60-second affairs, but longer 'deep burrow' visits sometimes occur, lasting several minutes.

The object of the earthworm's desire will then reciprocate the visit, each earthworm moving back and forth between each other's burrow openings like giddy teenagers.[32] While surface-dwelling earthworms don't have burrows to visit, they also seem to have a courtship ritual – Tiger worms' prospective partners have been observed repeatedly caressing each other, with short, gentle touches, before mating.[33] The pre-sex courtship ritual can last anything from a few minutes to an hour, before they get down to business. When they're ready to mate, the two earthworms lie next to each other facing in opposite directions – head to tail – glued together in a tight embrace with a sticky mucus produced by the clitellum. There, they'll stay stuck together in a sexual marathon that can last anything from one to three hours. Other earthworms will sometimes come up and touch the couple mid-act, an unwelcome interruption that can shorten the length of mating but doesn't stop the process. Charles Darwin was struck by the ardour of earthworm lovemaking; their passions, he wrote, were 'strong enough to overcome... their dread of light'.

Passionate they may be, but monogamous they are not; for most species of earthworm, multiple partners are common. And there's a darker side to these creatures' sex lives. To improve an earthworm's chance of success, it has an alarming secret weapon. Scientists have noticed that the Common earthworm has special setae (see also pages 91 and 94) on its body that it stabs into its mate's body during sex. These dagger-like bristles pierce the mate, damaging its skin, and inject a hormone that seems to improve the chance of the earthworm's sperm being accepted by the mate and lengthen the time before the mate searches for another lover.[34]

The clitellum is absolutely crucial to the whole mating process. The sticky mucus it produces, which initially glues the worms together so they can mate, hardens into a collar that slips forwards along each earthworm, collecting the other worm's sperm and their own eggs along the way. This mucus-collar eventually slides off the worm's head, both ends of the collar seal up, and it dries into a tiny lemon-shaped cocoon, which can nourish and protect the baby earthworms as they grow inside.

Depending on the species, earthworms repeatedly mate throughout the year. The Common earthworm, which is deep burrowing, will only produce about ten or so cocoons a year but smaller, surface-dwelling earthworms mate vigorously and frequently, producing as many as a hundred

Did you know

Observations from commercial worm breeders have even noted earthworm threesomes among *Eisenia andrei* (a close relative of the Tiger worm) and interbreeding between different species such as *E. fetida*, *E. andrei* and *E. hortensis* (the European night crawler), although this rare cross-species sex seems to result in infertile cocoons.

cocoons in one year. This might be because worms living nearer the surface are more prone to drought and predators. In general, however, earthworms in temperate countries tend to mate more frequently in spring (March/April) and autumn (September/October) when the weather is neither scorching hot nor freezing cold, a habit observed as early as the 1780s when the magazine *The Monthly Review, Or Literary Journal, Enlarged* noted: '... the common earth-worm propagates its species above ground, when the weather is mild and moist or the earth dewy.'[35]

Some species of earthworms don't even need a mate. Some are parthenogenetic, which means that they just have female reproductive organs but don't need a male to fertilise their eggs. Some earthworms, being hermaphroditic, choose to self-fertilise, and bend in half to impregnate themselves, a strategy that can help if an earthworm struggles to find a mate. Tiger worms self-fertilise about 10 per cent of the time.

CAN YOU TRAIN A WORM?

I would not enter on my list of friends,
(Tho' grac'd with polish'd manners and fine sense,
Yet wanting sensibility) the man
Who needlessly sets foot upon a worm.

William Cowper, *The Task* (1785)

Earthworms have been exposed to some fairly unpleasant experiments in the name of research. One, conducted back in the 1960s, tried to determine whether Common earthworms (*Lumbricus terrestris*) showed any capacity for learning.[36] The experiment involved a maze. The earthworms had to try and navigate the maze, while being exposed to light, heat and electric shocks as stimuli. Electric shocks were dished out as punishment for the worm making 'incorrect choices', i.e. going the wrong way, while the reward was being returned to the safety of the home container.

The experiment was designed to see whether the earthworms would *learn* how to get through the maze based on good or bad 'memories' of their choices. And whether they could repeat the puzzle time after time.

Incredibly, the experiment showed that the earthworms were indeed learning how to navigate their way through the maze. Not only that, but the frequency at which they made correct choices actually increased with each subsequent test. So, the earthworms got better and better at remembering their way through the maze with each run. After a two-week break, however, the earthworms 'forgot' their routes and, as the researcher noted: 'All changes in the earthworm which are produced in these experiments are transient by mammalian standards. After 15 days of rest, the performance of a highly trained [earthworm] is indistinguishable from an experimentally naïve one.'

DO EARTHWORMS SLEEP?

The answer to this question depends on how you define sleep. Some people describe it as a physiological state, which includes things such as altered consciousness, brainwave patterns consistent with sleep, reduction in sensory activity, sporadic eye movements or relaxed muscles. It's a definition that works well when applied to mammals, but for creatures who don't have such complex bodies or brains, a simpler behavioural definition is more useful.

If we talk about sleep as a behaviour, then we look for signs such as lack of movement, slowing down of normal function or non-responsiveness to external stimuli over the period of a twenty-four-hour day (longer periods of 'sleep' than twenty-four hours tend to be classified as hibernation or dormancy). Using the behavioural definition of sleep, earthworms do seem to have a period in the day when they rest. Research with the Common earthworm (*Lumbricus terrestris*), for example, has shown that they're super busy from dusk until dawn but that during daylight hours their oxygen consumption drops, indicating a period of slowdown.

DON'T USE CHEMICALS

- Earthworms have tolerated decades of pesticide use but their ability to detoxify themselves of harmful chemicals comes at a cost – soil that is regularly sprayed with pesticides seems to produce earthworms that are smaller in size and less able to reproduce (see *Are Earthworms in trouble?* page 22).

- Aim for a pesticide-free garden: healthy soil makes for healthy plants, which in turn are more able to resist disease; attract more beneficial insects (which eat garden pests); and look into natural pest solutions such as companion planting, organic sprays or biological control (such as nematodes).

DO EARTHWORMS
MAKE ANY NOISES?

Tucked away in the back pages of the *New York Times* for 5 August 1925 is an extraordinary, tiny snippet of news. The headline hails the news 'SAYS EARTH WORMS SING' and reads as follows:

> 'German Professor Finds They Emit Sounds of a Soprano Pitch. FREIBERG, Germany, Aug. 4 –Professor Mangold, a German teacher of zoology, says that he has discovered accidentally that earthworms can sing. He placed a dozen earthworms under a glass cover in carrying out certain experiments and to his surprise rhythmical [sic] sounds of soprano pitch emanated from the container. The savant insists that an investigation showed the music came from the earthworms.'

Mangold was the first scientist to suggest that earthworms make sounds. Two years later, in 1927, another academic, Rudolf Ruedemann – fascinated by Mangold's observations – asserted in *Science* that, based on his own personal experiences, 'American earthworms also produce sound'. He noted '...on a sultry May evening [...] earthworms in our garden back of the house could be distinctly heard. Being incredulous at first, I sat quietly on a chair until

I also heard an exceedingly fine rasping noise all around me. It was a chorus of almost unbelievably small voices in the dark [...] We have since heard the singing every year, always on warm spring evenings about and after dusk.'[37]

Where these two eminent men differed, however, was in their theories as to how the earthworms made their sounds. Mangold believed the sound to come from their mouths, while Ruedemann suggested it was the earthworms drawing their bristly setae over some hard object near the entrance to their burrows, possibly as a way of attracting a mate.

The mystery of the 'singing' earthworms has yet to be solved and little research has been done into the sounds earthworms make, if any. Farmers who breed worms for vermiculture have been known to record 'popping' sounds coming from their compost bins, while the Nage people of the eastern Indonesian island of Flores have long maintained that a species of earthworm in their local environment makes a 'croaking' noise.[38]

Of the sounds that have been recorded, however, one of the most likely explanations for earthworm sounds is, at least in part, their movement through soil. Sound waves are produced when small grains of organic matter move or rub against each other, or when small cracks are created in the soil. Depending on the size and number of earthworms, the noise may be considerable. David Attenborough, in his memoir *Life on Air*, remembers the extraordinary underground noises made when he was filming the Giant Gippsland earthworm in Australia. He compares the loud squelching noise, caused by the earthworm dragging its body through the wet soil, to the noise of a toilet: 'as you walk through the South Australian meadows you may hear, immediately behind you, what sounds like someone flushing a lavatory.'[39]

DO EARTHWORMS
MAKE FRIENDS?

They perhaps have a trace of social feeling, for they
are not disturbed by crawling over each other's
bodies, and sometimes lie in contact.

Charles Darwin, *The Formation of Vegetable Mould through
the Action of Worms, with Observations on their Habits* (1881)

A re earthworms sociable? It seems an extraordinary
question to ask of an animal that is effectively just
a tube with a mouth and bum, and yet a recent scientific
experiment suggests that the lowly worm has a much more
sophisticated communal life than was ever imagined.

At a Belgian university, researchers discovered that Tiger
worms (*Eisenia fetida*) used touch to communicate with each
other and influence each other's behaviour. By using touch,
the earthworms formed 'herds', which then all travelled
together as a group in the same direction.

In one experiment, a cluster of forty earthworms were
placed in a chamber of soil that had two identical chambers
branching off it. Scientists expected that the earthworms
would evenly distribute themselves among the soil, but
instead they moved as a group, all ending up in one chamber

together. Repeated tests showed the same 'herding' pattern.

But how did the earthworms decide as a group which chamber to move to? To test whether the earthworms were using chemical signals or touch to communicate, researchers created a maze, which the earthworms had to navigate. If individual earthworms travelled by themselves, they went via different routes through the maze. The fact that they didn't follow each other suggested that the worms weren't navigating by any kind of chemical trail left by the worm in front.

However, when two worms travelled together, they stayed together on the journey and ended up at the same destination. By crossing bodies or rubbing next to each other, the earthworms seemed to communicate through social cues and end up in the same place. Researchers also noticed that the earthworms often clustered together into compact groups when they were out of the soil, and suspect that many other species of earthworm may follow similar patterns of behaviour.

Quite why earthworms seem to form 'herds' is a question yet to be answered. One theory is that grouping into clusters – as is the case with many different animals

– offers a greater level of protection from predators such as flatworms.

Earthworms also like to socialise in the evenings. Under the cover of darkness, they come to the top of their own burrows and investigate their neighbours. Gripping on to its own burrow with its tail, the earthworm will poke its head into the entrance of a neighbouring burrow, seeking a potential mate (see *How do Earthworms have sex?* page 113).

DO EARTHWORMS TAKE RISKS?

It's easy to imagine that the life of an earthworm is fairly sedate. And yet, like many species, they are known to take risks. For most of the time, creatures survive by avoiding dangerous situations. Under certain circumstances, however, such as lack of food, risk-taking may be the only option to give an animal a fighting chance.

While this is an easy behaviour to observe in large mammals, no one had thought that an animal as simple as an earthworm would make calculated decisions in the face of difficulty. One recent study,[40] however, proved that the Common earthworm (*Lumbricus terrestris*) took risks in the face of starvation. In the experiment, scientists took three groups of earthworms (non-starved, half-starved, and fully starved) and presented them with two foraging choices. The high-risk choice had lots of food but was in bright light – which is harmful to earthworms; the low-risk choice had little food but was nice and dark. The fully starved and extremely hungry group of earthworms not only selected the high-risk food more often than the other two groups, but also made their choices quicker than the others. Earthworms, it seems, are prepared to risk the threat of predators and desiccation from daylight if food sources dwindle.

HOW LONG DO EARTHWORMS LIVE?

While the angels, all pallid, and wan,
Uprising, unveiling, affirm
That the play is the tragedy, 'Man,'
And its hero, the Conqueror Worm.

Edgar Allen Poe, 'The Conqueror Worm' (1843)

There does seem to be some correlation between how deep an earthworm lives in the soil and how long it'll last. Surface dwellers are relatively short-lived – one to three years – but reproduce frequently and easily, so populations quickly recover. Shallow burrowers have a greater life expectancy – up to five years – but it's the deep burrowers who can reach the impressive age of ten years or more. They only lay a few cocoons a year, so the downside is that populations are quickly decimated if the soil is disturbed. Left to their own devices, however, and with plenty to eat, deep-burrowing earthworms can live well into their teens.

DO EARTHWORMS
EXPERIENCE PAIN?

No creature is too bulky or formidable for
man's destructive energies—none too minute
and insignificant for his keen detection and skill
of capture. It was ordained from the beginning
that we should be the masters and subduers
of all inferior animals. Let us remember,
however, that we ourselves, like the creatures
we slay, subjugate, and modify, are ... temporary
sojourners here, and co-tenants with the worm
and the whale of one small planet.

Sir Richard Owen, Lecture to the London Society of Arts,
The Raw Materials of the Animal Kingdom (1852)

This is a tricky one. It can be difficult to tell if an animal is experiencing pain, especially if there is no verbal communication. Also, scientists don't agree on what pain is. When a worm is wriggling on a hook, for example, is this just an unconscious reflex or something more akin to pain as we experience it?

All animals have something called *nociception*. This is a capacity to react to harmful things. Through their neural systems, all animals react to dangerous or noxious stimuli, in order to avoid being either damaged or killed. This capacity is partly based on unconscious reflexes, rather than necessarily a conscious experience.

So, when a worm wriggles at the end of a hook, is it just the creature automatically reacting in some way but not actually experiencing pain in the same way we do? The debate rages on. Some scientists insist that earthworms don't feel pain but instead are simply responding, mechanically, to a harmful stimulus (in the same way we might close our eyes to a bright source of light). Others aren't so sure.

Researchers who challenge this notion look for other signs that would suggest an animal is in distress. Earthworms have been shown to produce two kinds of chemical – enkephalins and beta endorphins – which are believed to help them endure pain.[42] If a creature produces painkilling chemicals, so the theory goes, it must be doing so in response to pain.

ADD MORE WORMS

• Often in new-build properties or 'instant gardens', if soil has been imported or moved from elsewhere on site, the earthworm population can be dramatically reduced or even completely eliminated. In this instance, it can be useful to buy in earthworms and introduce them to the soil. While it can be tempting to buy a bag of earthworms and hope for the best, unless you first improve the soil conditions the new residents won't survive.

• Most commercial worm farms recommend that you improve the soil before you add new earthworms to a plot, ideally leaving the manure, compost, leaf mould or other organic material to 'season' and begin to decay for a year before introducing earthworms (*see How to help earthworms #1* page 28).

- When the plot is ready for its new arrivals, how you introduce the earthworms will depend on the species. Deep- and shallow-burrowing earthworms, for example, will need 'digging in' – scoop out the soil to a trowel's depth, pop them in and then cover them over again.

- Or even better, you can buy colonies of mixed worms (deep and shallow burrowers but not surface dwellers/compost worms) in biodegradable boxes; you simply dig a hole and bury the entire box, water it and cover it with soil, and the earthworms will slowly work their way out of the box and into the surrounding soil, getting used to the new conditions as they go. Within no time, the earthworms should be settling in, mating and going on to repopulate your garden soil and bring it back to health.

Whether this pain is like the sensation we feel, we don't know, but it's an interesting avenue to explore.

The idea that earthworms might experience pain isn't a new one, however; nor is the notion that we should not willingly inflict harm on them. In an article written by a Reverend Ljunggren for the *New York Times* in 1931, he recalls the experiments of a Swedish professor who wanted to establish whether earthworms felt pain. His tests, which involved electrical shocks, convinced the professor that earthworms were, indeed, capable of feeling pain and he spent the rest of his career trying to persuade anglers not to use earthworms as bait. 'The good professor,' wrote Rev. Ljunggren, 'filled with compassion for the thousands of poor worms that were impaled annually upon fishermen's hooks, went on a lecture tour to try and persuade [them] to discard the worm as bait. But they merely smiled and continued to halt their hooks as their fathers had done, and as no doubt, their descendants will continue to do.'[40]

ENDNOTES

1. Natural England Commissioned Report NECR145: 'Earthworms in England: distribution, abundance and habitats' (2014): http://publications.naturalengland.org.uk/publication/5174957155811328.

2. Lowe, C.N., 'Interactions within earthworm communities: A laboratory-based approach with potential applications for soil restoration', University Of Central Lancashire, Faculty Of Science (April 2000): core.ac.uk/download/pdf/9632799.pdf.

3. Butt, K.R. et al., 'An oasis of fertility on a barren island: Earthworms at Papadil, Isle of Rum', *The Glasgow Naturalist* (2016) Volume 26, Part 2, pp. 13–20.

4. Meentemeyer, V. et al., 'World patterns and amounts of terrestrial plant litter production', *BioScience* 32(2), (1982), pp. 125–128.

5. Xiao, Z. et al., 'Earthworms affect plant growth and resistance against herbivores: A meta-analysis', *Functional Ecology* (18 August 2017).

6. Zaller, J.G. et al., 'Herbivory of an invasive slug is affected by earthworms and the composition of plant communities', *BMC Ecology* 13, 20 (2013): https://doi.org/10.1186/1472-6785-13-20.

7. Decaëns, T. et al., 'Seed dispersal by surface casting activities of earthworms in Colombian grasslands', *Acta Oecologica* 24(4) (2003), pp. 175–185.

8. Dann, L., 'Major survey finds worms are rare or absent in 40% of fields', *Farmers Weekly* (22 February 2019): www.fwi.co.uk/arable/land-preparation/soils/major-survey-finds-worms-are-rare-or-absent-in-20-of-fields.

9. Kanianska, R. et al., 'Assessment of Relationships between Earthworms and Soil Abiotic and Biotic Factors as a Tool in Sustainable Agricultural', *Sustainability* 8 (9): 906 (7 September 2016).

10. Scheer, R. and Moss, D., 'Dirt Poor: Have Fruits and Vegetables Become Less Nutritious?', *Scientific American* (27 April 2011).

11. Givaudan, N. et al., 'Acclimation of earthworms to chemicals in anthropogenic landscapes, physiological mechanisms and soil ecological implications', *Soil Biology and Biochemistry* 73 (2014), pp. 49–58: DOI: 10.1016/j.soilbio.2014.01.032

12. The National Severe Storms Laboratory, Severe Weather 101: Flood Basics: www.nssl.noaa.gov/education/svrwx101/floods

13. Xiaofeng Jiang et al., 'Toxicological effects of polystyrene microplastics on earthworm (Eisenia fetida)', *Environmental Pollution* 259 (April 2020).

14. Paoletti, M.G. et al., 'Nutrient content of earthworms consumed byYe'kuana Amerindians of the Alto Orinoco of Venezuela', Proceedings of the Royal Society of London. Series B: Biological SciencesVolume 270, Issue 1512 (07 February 2003)

15. Cianferoni, A., et al., 'Visceral Larva Migrans Associated With Earthworm Ingestion: Clinical Evolution in an Adolescent Patient', *Pediatrics* 117(2): e336–e339 (1 August 2006).

16. Reynolds, J.W. and Reynolds, W.M., 'Earthworms in Medicine', *American Journal of Nursing* 72(7):1273 (August 1972).

17. Mira Grdisa, M., 'Therapeutic Properties of Earthworms' in *Bioremediation, Biodiversity and Bioavailability*, Global Science Books (2013): http://www.globalsciencebooks.info/Online/GSBOnline/images/2013/BBB_7(1)/BBB_7(1)1-5o.pdf

18. Chuang, S. et al., 'Influence of ultraviolet radiation on selected physiological responses of earthworms', *Journal of Experimental Biology* 209 (2006), pp. 4304–4312: doi: 10.1242/jeb.02521.

19. Seymour, M.K., 'Locomotion and Coelomic Pressure in *Lumbricus terrestris* L', *Journal of Experimental Biology* 51 (1969), pp. 47–58.

20. Quillin, K.J., 'Kinematic scaling of locomotion by hydrostatic animals: ontogeny of peristaltic crawling by the earthworm lumbricus terrestris', *Journal of Experimental Biology* 202 (1999), pp. 661–674.

21. Zhang, D. et al., 'Earthworm epidermal mucus: Rheological behavior reveals drag-reducing characteristics in soil', *Soil and Tillage Research* 158 (May 2016), pp. 57–66.

22. Verdes, A. & Gruber, D.F., 'Glowing Worms: Biological, Chemical, and Functional Diversity of Bioluminescent Annelids', *Integrative and Comparative Biology* 57(1), (July 2017), pp. 18–32.

23. Samuelson, J., *Humble Creatures* (John Van Voorst, London, 1858).

24. Montgomerie, R. and Weatherhead, P.J., 'How robins find worms', *Animal Behaviour* 54 (1997), pp. 143–151.

25. Cranfield University, 'Earthworm population triples with use of cover crops' (25 September 2019): https://phys.org/news/2019-09-earthworm-population-triples-crops.html.

26. Liebeke, M. et al., 'Unique metabolites protect earthworms against plant polyphenols', *Nature Communications* 6:7869 (2015): doi: 10.1038/ncomms8869.

27. Pfiffner, L., 'Earthworms – Architects of fertile soils', Order no. 1629, International edition © FiBL Research Institute of Organic Agriculture FiBL (2014).

28. Nuutinen, V. and Butt, K.R., 'Homing ability widens the sphere of influence of the earthworm *Lumbricus terrestris* L', *Soil Biology and Biochemistry* 37:4 (April 2005), pp. 805–807.

29. *The Monthly Review, Or Literary Journal*, Volume LXII (1810).

30. Usherwood, J., 'A New Twist On Underground Eating', *Journal Of Experimental Biology* 209:23 (2006): Vi Doi: 10.1242/Jeb.02575.

31. Penning, K.A. and Wrigley, D.M. 'Aged *Eisenia fetida* earthworms exhibit decreased reproductive success', *Invertebrate Reproduction & Development*, 62:2 (2018), pp. 67–73.

32. Nuutinen, V. and Butt, K.R., 'The mating behaviour of the earthworm *Lumbricus terrestris* (Oligochaeta: Lumbricidae)', *Journal of Zoology* 242:4 (August 1997), pp. 783–798.

33. Grove, A.J. and Cowley, L.F., 'Memoirs: On the Reproductive Processes of the Brandling Worm, Eisenia Foetida. (Sav.)', *Journal Of Cell Science* (1926) s2-70: pp. 559–581.

34. Koene, J.M., et al., 'Piercing the partner's skin influences sperm uptake in the earthworm Lumbricus Terrestris', *Behavioral Ecology and Sociobiology*, 59:2 (2005), pp. 243–249.

35. 'Letters and Papers on Agriculture, Planting &c.' in *The Monthly Review, Or Literary Journal, Enlarged*, 1780.

36. Greene Datta, L., 'Learning in the Earthworm, *Lumbricus Terrestris*', *The American Journal Of Psychology* 75:4 (December 1962), pp. 531–553.

37. Ruedemann, R., '"Singing" Earthworms', *Science* 65:1676 (11 February 1927), p. 163.

38. Forth, G., *Why the Porcupine is Not a Bird: Explorations in the Folk Zoology of an Eastern Indonesian People* (University of Toronto Press, 2016).

39. Attenborough, D., *Life on Air* (BBC Books, 2003) p. 394.

40. Sandhu, P. et al., 'Worms make risky choices too: the effect of starvation on foraging in the common earthworm (*Lumbricus terrestris*)', *Canadian Journal of Zoology*, 96 (2018), pp. 1278–1283.

41. Alumets, J. et al., 'Neuronal localisation of immunoreactive enkephalin and ß-endorphin in the earthworm', *Nature* 279 (1979), pp. 805–806.

42. Ljunggren, Rev. C.J., 'Earthworms Feel Pain', *New York Times* (20 September 1931).